TRAIN
YOUR
BRAIN

TRAIN
YOUR
BRAIN

How to Build a Million Dollar Business in Record Time

DANA WILDE

BALBOA.
PRESS

A DIVISION OF HAY HOUSE

Balboa Press books may be ordered through booksellers or by contacting:

Balboa Press
A Division of Hay House
1663 Liberty Drive
Bloomington, IN 47403
www.balboapress.com
1-(877) 407-4847

Because of the dynamic nature of the Internet, any web addresses or links contained in this book may have changed since publication and may no longer be valid. The views expressed in this work are solely those of the author and do not necessarily reflect the views of the publisher, and the publisher hereby disclaims any responsibility for them.

The author of this book does not dispense medical advice or prescribe the use of any technique as a form of treatment for physical, emotional, or medical problems without the advice of a physician, either directly or indirectly. The intent of the author is only to offer information of a general nature to help you in your quest for emotional and spiritual well-being. In the event you use any of the information in this book for yourself, which is your constitutional right, the author and the publisher assume no responsibility for your actions.

Any people depicted in stock imagery provided by Thinkstock are models, and such images are being used for illustrative purposes only. Certain stock imagery © Thinkstock.

ISBN: 978-1-4525-7156-0 (sc)
ISBN: 978-1-4525-7158-4 (hc)
ISBN: 978-1-4525-7157-7 (e)

Library of Congress Control Number: 2013905911

Printed in the United States of America.

Balboa Press rev. date: 8/5/2013

TABLE OF CONTENTS

Part 2
Mindware Experiments

ABOUT THIS BOOK

This Train Your Brain book is divided into two learning parts: Part 1 is all about the concept, the basic information; Part 2 is a series of 20 fun exercises which help you apply the principles and ideas in Part 1. They are called **Mindware Experiments** and can be found at the back of this book. These simple and thoughtful exercises are guaranteed to engage you and bring you immediate results!

You have three options when reading this book:

1) Read all of Part 1 straight through for an overview, then do each of the 20 exercises,

2) Read the chapters in Part 1 and participate in each of the **Mindware Experiments** as they appear; or,

3) Read Part 1 straight through, re-read again and this time participate in each experiment as it appears, in order and in context.

Also, you may want to visit http://www.trainyourbrainformore.com and download a FREE workbook that you can use in conjunction with this book.

When you understand Train Your Brain, you'll know why our recommendation is to follow whichever option "feels good" to you at the time. We know you will know what to do and there's no right or wrong way.

Finally . . . before we dig into the wonderful thing we call the human brain, I want to say the most important thing on this joyous ride is to . . .

HAVE FUN!

CHAPTER 1

WHAT IS GOING ON HERE?

Many years ago, in the early 90's, I watched an HBO documentary, part of its **America Undercover** series, which examined the lives of persons with "Multiple Personality Disorder," a rare medical affliction known today as Dissociative Identity Disorder, or DID.

Up until that point I knew the brain was incredibly powerful, but what I learned in this documentary really blew my mind and opened up a whole new level of understanding that really, the only limits we have are those limits which we put on ourselves.

I clearly remember being astounded and enlightened by what I learned. In particular, the amazing story of Barb, a 35-year-old woman with four or five different personalities living inside her brain.

I remember sitting on my couch watching HBO's film crew follow Barb as she grocery shops with her husband and two girls. Initially, Barb is interacting and speaking with her family in a normal way, chatting with her husband, and letting her two eager daughters pick out their favorite cereals.

Everything seems quite typical, nothing out of the ordinary but, after a few moments, something odd happens. After letting her two daughters pick

1

out their favorite cereals, Barb informs her husband of a strawberry cereal she especially wants for herself. What struck me at the time was hearing Barb ask for her favorite cereal in a distinctly "child-like" voice.

The narrator of the documentary quickly informs viewers that Barb is slipping into an alter personality, that of a five-year-old girl named Mae. This is typical behavior for Barb, we're told, who often "slips into and out of" many different personalities.

And as Barb continues looking for her favorite strawberry cereal, something even more extraordinary happens. After a brief moment scanning the shelf, Barb acts as if she's having a hard time seeing and, looking at her husband, she says she can't see with "Barb's" glasses on.

Gently accommodating his wife, he helps remove the glasses and "Mae," the five year-old girl momentarily living inside Barb, can now pick out her favorite strawberry cereal.

Apparently, as Barb "slips" into the personality of a five-year-old girl, her eyesight does the same. I remember immediately thinking, "Is this for real?"

Is this woman's eyesight literally changing between personalities? Does Barb actually see better when she slips into the personality of the five-year-old girl? I was completely floored by this possibility!

Unfortunately, the documentary didn't say whether Barb's eyesight had, in fact, literally changed. But I wanted to know! I mean, was there a physiological reason for the dramatic change in Barb's eyesight? Or was her mind playing tricks on her? Was this amazing incident real?

Whatever the case, I was certain Barb's story, at least the story I was experiencing, had an answer. I was sure of it.

So I became inspired by the prospect of piecing together the whys and hows of Barb's amazing story. I committed myself to finding some kind of an answer. I gathered as much information as I could on the subject of DID. And, boy, I'll tell you, I gathered some amazing stuff!

First, imagine a "split" in the brain allowing persons with DID to "believe at the deepest level" that two or more individual personalities actually live inside their bodies. I know this sounds a bit otherworldly for many people, but this is what life is actually like for persons living with DID.

And because I do many workshops on the brain, I've talked with people who've attended workshops on DID. In fact, many people have sent me articles or books on this fascinating subject. For me, nothing reveals the power of the brain more than the amazing stories we hear from people with Dissociative Identity Disorder. Why is it so amazing?

For starters, different personalities in a person with DID might have different ages, or distinct sets of personality traits, and even unique handwriting styles . . . which I later found out to be pretty typical stuff for those with DID . . . I also heard some mind-blowing stories!

Now keep in mind, these are all medically documented cases . . .

- One personality has a scar or bruise on the body but when the person slips into a different personality . . . the scar vanishes!
- One personality is able to drink orange juice without any problems, while another personality becomes allergic to the orange juice and breaks out in hives!
- One personality has green eyes and another personality has brown or blue eyes!

It's just amazing! The list goes on and on. Again, all are **medically proven.**

In all my research, I found the gem I was looking for . . .

. . . an answer to Barb's story!

Incredibly enough, I learned there are people with DID who have differing levels of visual perception between the various personalities. There are many documented cases, where one personality in a person with DID might need to wear prescription glasses, while another personality in the same person tests out with perfect 20/20 vision.

I knew something astounding was happening inside that woman's mind!

It's beyond belief. And what's even more amazing about people like Barb is that doctors basically have very few answers for this incredible DID phenomenon. Mysteries of the brain are still baffling our most brilliant minds. Thousands of years of medical technology, and yet what we don't know!

Thanks to documentaries like HBO's and the numerous books on the subject of the brain, we're all finding out more every day that our minds are much more powerful than we ever imagined and nothing drove home this point more for me than the incredible cases of people with DID. It's so clear that what we can accomplish with our brain has no limits and we're going to continue to drive that point home in this book.

CHAPTER 2

THE ROAD TO SUCCESS BEGINS AND ENDS IN YOUR MIND

Welcome. If you're reading this book, you've decided to "train" your brain. Good, because the real road to your success—family, personal or financial success—begins and ends in your mind.

By making small changes in the way you think—thinking in new and more constructive ways—you can literally train your brain to control *every* aspect of your life.

I created Train Your Brain to give you the tools to produce results, which *last*. I've learned that anyone and everyone can be successful. And I also know firsthand creating success that isn't going to fizzle out can be accomplished quickly and effortlessly by making Train Your Brain part of your daily regimen.

Although no one truly believes success can be achieved without some good effort on our part, we all want it to be *more effortless*. I know, more than anything, most people want to be in *control* of their own success. And the only way to achieve this sense of control is to create your own method for success from inside your own mind.

Generally speaking, traditional approaches to training for entrepreneurs and small business owners appear in one of two forms.

The first are *action-based* trainings. These are "how to" trainings. They teach you how to market, how to network, how to make phone calls, how to organize, how to bring your business online, and so on. They focus on "action" or "how to" as the method to success.

There is nothing inherently wrong with action-based training. We feature a lot of action-based trainers on The Mind Aware Show and of course we all want to put systems in place that help to streamline our success, but there are two inherent drawbacks to these types of of training materials.

First, many action-based trainings are "time-intensive" which means finding more time in our already busy lives, which results in a much heavier workload and usually adds stress.

Many of us have had the experience of attending a seminar or training where the presenter is really convincing, with all the "latest and greatest" methods for business growth. They explain some new process or system or marketing technique you should be implementing in your business that will increase your sales or grow your business in some way. And you get super-excited about how the new systems will increase your productivity and bring you more money.

However, many times when you begin adding all of the new tasks to your already-full schedule, you soon find you're working more hours than ever, and pretty soon you're feeling overwhelmed and stressed out. And rule number one in Train Your Brain is that feeling overwhelmed and stressed out is counter-productive to success.

The other downside to action-based trainings is they perpetuate the illusion that our success or growth in our business is because of hard work.

What you will learn in Train Your Brain is that hard work doesn't equal big money. Some of the hardest working people in our society are some of the lowest paid. Others who seem to do nothing at all or at the very least do only what seems like "fun" are some of the highest paid. You'll learn that you truly can make more while working less.

Just to be clear, I know and expect that you will take some action to grow your business and you will learn exactly the type of action I recommend. I call it Intentional Action and I'll explain in it great detail in this book. However, you will grow your business faster and easier when you really understand that changing the way you think is the only way to attain that next level.

In addition to traditional action-based trainings offered to small business owners, at the other end of the spectrum are *motivational or inspirational* trainings. Here the main objective is to get you "fired up." Again, there is nothing inherently wrong with being motivated or inspired. I mean, who doesn't like to be "fired up"? However, again, there are some major drawbacks to these types of trainings.

When you attend a motivational training, you come out of this training all charged-up and ready to take on the world but, unfortunately, that excitement doesn't last. In a short period of time it loses its punch. I call it the "Snicker bar effect." It's the same kind of letdown as when the initial rush of sugar subsides after you eat a candy bar. The buzz . . . the boost . . . whatever you want to call it, is gone and you're not really left with any "usable" information that you can apply to your business.

So, the simpler alternative to labor-intensive action-based trainings and the more lasting alternative to short-lived motivational trainings is Train Your Brain. It combines the best from both of these camps to create a program, which leads to simpler and more lasting success.

Train Your Brain begins with awareness and it trains you to shift your mindset.

In fact, I believe this mindset shift is so important to business success and personal fulfillment that I named my show, The Mind Aware.

Many of us are running our businesses and our lives on "auto-pilot." And we're letting our unconscious minds make our decisions for us. Unfortunately, when we run our lives on autopilot, our results suffer. But guess what? This is reversible. It is totally possible to change. It's possible to change our minds and our results.

A big part of Train Your Brain's effectiveness is that its techniques help you to build up your awareness but, in order to do so, you must first choose to do so. The choice I'm talking about is the choice to make a conscious effort to get your mind aware. It's the choice to change your old ways of thinking which have become obstacles to your success. It's the choice to create a new future for yourself.

So if you've been wondering why others are more successful than you . . . it's only because you haven't yet learned the big part your brain plays in creating success, that's all.

But you will. You will realize there are no magical ways to be successful. No Midas touch. No special qualities you must possess. In the end, you will realize being "smarter" than everyone else or "working harder" than everyone else has no bearing on your success.

However, I believe the most exciting part of your Train Your Brain journey is that you'll discover you have exactly what it does take to be successful! You'll discover anyone can be successful!

I created Train Your Brain to give you the tools to produce results, which last. I've learned that anyone and everyone can be successful. And I also know firsthand creating lasting success can be accomplished quickly and effortlessly by making Train Your Brain part of your daily regimen.

Although no one truly believes success can be achieved without some effort on our part, we all want it to be more effortless. I know, more than anything, most people want to be in control of their own success. And the only way to achieve this sense of control is to create it from inside your own mind.

Overall, you will learn how to leverage the power of your mind, so you will feel more positive, confident, and sure about the actions you are taking in your business and your life . . . and those actions will create success so easily, it will feel effortless.

Get ready for this amazing journey that takes you from where you are to where you want to be!

CHAPTER 3

RISING TO THE TOP: THE MILLION DOLLAR CLUB

Some of you may already be familiar with me, and my work. You may know me from my years as a field leader in the direct sales industry; or as an independent trainer and speaker at conferences and workshops for entrepreneurs; or as host of The Mind Aware teleseminar series for direct sellers; or as the host of The Mind Aware Radio Show for entrepreneurs and small business owners. On the other hand, some of you may not be familiar with me at all, so I'd like to give you a little background.

Prior to my involvement working with and training entrepreneurs and business owners, I lived a full life, exploring many different industries and occupations. I began by working in corporate America, and decided quite quickly this was not for me. I spent many years working as a writer and published author. I lived overseas for most of a decade and spent several years in Japan, Vietnam, and other parts of Asia. Finally I worked in the film and video industry and enjoyed a fruitful career as a award-winning writer, producer, and script supervisor.

Then one day, like millions of people worldwide, I discovered a direct sales product I would later go on to sell. I became so excited about this product after attending an in-home party that I immediately requested material on how to become a "consultant" or "distributor."

This product was sold via party plan, and I talked to so many people about my new venture that before my distributor kit even arrived I had already booked three parties. Maybe you've heard the term "ignorance on fire"? That was me. I didn't have a clue what I was doing, but I was sure doing it with lots of energy and enthusiasm!

Now many of you know that part of being successful in direct sales has to do with offering other people the same business opportunity you were offered and helping them to be successful in their businesses.

As I was looking for trainings for my team members, I could see there was nothing outside of either "how to", action-based trainings or short-lived motivational trainings. I felt like I was sitting on this wealth of knowledge about how the brain worked and I wanted to teach what I knew about the brain to my team members.

So, within the first few months of my direct sales career, I wrote Train Your Brain and I taught it to my team members. While it's much more common today to talk about things like the power of positive thinking, at the time, it was a bit of a leap for them to embrace it. But they did embrace it and apply it and as a team, we effortlessly rose to the million-dollar level.

The Million Dollar Club was comprised of leaders whose teams (within three levels) sold one million dollars or more during the calendar year. With an average product price point of around $20, this really was quite an achievement. When I joined the company, less than 15 members made up the illustrious Million Dollar Club, and attaining that level seemed like a pretty daunting task. But, like I said, I certainly saw myself getting there.

Most of those already in the Million Dollar Club spent many years working before they eventually got in. So, naturally, everyone was surprised when I purchased my kit, became a new distributor one day and just 19 months later became a full-fledged member of the Million Dollar Club!

And the team I'd built didn't just break the previous company record for rise to the Million Dollar Club. We shattered it! The previous record was roughly 42 months! In fact, not one team has ever come close to reaching this milestone, and our record still stands today.

However, even more importantly, it was because of this work with my team members that I realized that these techniques could be taught and that it is easy for anyone to change their mindset if they know how.

Eventually I went on to sell my direct sales business and "semi-retire". I spent a year reading, gardening, and studying. I studied hypnotherapy, but I kept getting requests for Train Your Brain. People requesting me to speak or train their team members and ultimately I realized there was a new mission for me, and that mission became The Mind Aware.

I founded The Mind Aware for the same reason I wrote Train Your Brain . . . there was a hole in the market with regards to the trainings offered to small business owners . . . entrepreneurs were trying to grow their businesses using "how-to" action based trainings and no one was teaching entrepreneurs how to leverage the power of their minds so they could have faster growth with less work and we wanted to fill that void with Train Your Brain and The Mind Aware.

As I write this, The Mind Aware has been in business for two years. We've grown from zero, not even having a product, to present day where we have over done over $1,000,000 in sales, we have 60,000 followers and countless success stories . . . and it's just the tip of the iceberg.

You may have heard the idea, "You need to *think* like a successful person in order to *be a* successful person" or, "You need to *think* like a rich person in order to become a rich person." Well because of my direct sales team members initially and later, the followers of The Mind Aware, I've discovered that you can *train* people to think in this manner.

Train Your Brain is built on the basic premise of Intentional Action—get your mindset right first and then take action! That is the "magic!"

Action alone has very little to do with success. The "actions" of our team during our record rise to the top were always preceded by thoughts and feelings generated by our own minds. I will go into great detail on the importance of thought and feeling in carrying out action in later chapters.

This is why I believe Train Your Brain is so effective. It is not relying on action alone. It's not singing the same old song about working harder and working longer. Conversely, it's also not telling you to sit in bed all day and think happy thoughts.

Train Your Brain is the total package. It will show you that the mind is the single, most important "tool" at your disposal, capable of bringing you whatever you want.

Train Your Brain shows that your intentions (your thoughts and feelings), and your actions (what you do) are not mutually exclusive. In other words, your thoughts and feelings must be combined with your actions in order for your actions to have the best chance for success.

Remember, Intentional Action—combining thoughts and feelings with action—is the bread and butter of Train Your Brain—providing you with a "stronger, quicker method" for success and resulting in the kind of success that lasts much longer for you.

Over the next few chapters, I want to keep explaining this material in the same way I learned it; continually laying the groundwork for how the mind "works" and how our brains can and will create their own success stories. And also, how you can easily "rebuild" and "reshape" your business and your life any way you want and know that it is not magic.

And so, to explain this information as I've learned it over the last 30 years, with each point building on the next, let's recap the concepts I've shared so far . . .

1. The brain is your largest and most valuable asset. Relying on yourself and using your own mind as the primary force for your success will create something much stronger and longer-lasting.

2. Motivational training can make you feel good, but typically these good feelings wear off. Also, the "elusive nature" of these trainings often makes them more difficult to apply to your day-to-day business.

3. Action or hard work alone will never guarantee your success. Many of us in network marketing and direct sales are working tirelessly and, in fact, likely working too much. While consistent action is important to your success . . . it is not the REASON for your success.

4. Finally, in reading this book, you will not merely be "learning" Train Your Brain methods. You will be implementing them, as well. And as you begin applying these techniques and the various Mindware Experiments to your business, you will

experience how quickly and dramatically it affects everything you do.

Don't take my word that Train Your Brain works. Practice the Mindware Experiments, and apply the fun, exciting techniques in this book and YOUR OWN RESULTS will be your proof of Train Your Brain's amazing effectiveness.

I promise . . .

You will experience your own success stories.

You will experience a "noticeable shift" in your business.

Train Your Brain will increase your business and transform your life!

CHAPTER 4

THE POWER OF THE MIND

I want to tell you a couple of stories about some amazing people who really bring to light the astonishing and miraculous power of the human mind.

The first one is Dr. Nicholas Hatsopoulos, a neuroscientist working at The University of Chicago. He wanted to find a way to help quadriplegics live a better life. From 2006-2008, he conducted numerous studies on the brain targeted at getting quadriplegics to function as close to normal as possible.

Dr. Hatsopolous' findings helped develop an implantable device and computer software that enabled quadriplegic patients to move cursors on a computer screen with ONLY their thoughts. I want to repeat that so the point is not lost. We now live in a day and age where something in our physical world, a computer cursor, can be moved with nothing more than a person's thoughts.

This revolutionary device, called Braingate, is helping many quadriplegics today. With little or no physical capabilities to speak of, these patients use their own minds and transform their lives, now accomplishing many of the same tasks as able-bodied people.

Isn't it miraculous? Being able to move a cursor on a computer screen with your own thoughts?

When I was a child this was the stuff of science fiction or wacky psychic reports. Moving objects with your mind was the type of things you'd hear about in ghost stories.

But nowadays we're hearing and seeing new examples of the limitless potential of the mind and how strong and powerful our thoughts can be nearly every day. The fields of quantum physics and quantum mechanics continue to grow all the time, and it seems as if we're entering new frontiers on a daily basis.

Another area of research I've always found fascinating is the connection between mind and body. Can our thoughts affect our body? Researchers are finding the answer is a resounding YES!

For example, as early as the late 1800s Dr. William Bates created The Bates Method, a series of exercises designed to strengthen eyesight without the use of corrective eyeglasses.

As a young teaching assistant at Columbia University in New York, Dr. Bates repeatedly encouraged his fellow doctors to throw away their glasses. As you can imagine, the people around him thought he was crazy and in fact, they eventually fired him!

Nevertheless, over the many years he worked at the hospital, Dr. Bates had found that eyesight was profoundly affected by "states of mind." Meaning, differences in vision or eyesight were often dependent on whether a person is anxious, confused, excited or relaxed.

Dr. Bates concluded vision problems could be easily corrected with a person's own mind and he put his findings to work. For years Dr. Bates helped many people reverse poor vision by combining eye-strengthening exercises while also focusing on emotional states.

In his book, The Natural Vision Improvement Kit, Dr. Meir Schneider tells how he used The Bates Method to reverse his own blindness. That's right . . . reverse.

You see, by the time he was seven years old, Meir Schneider was certified as legally blind. Performing all his schoolwork and reading in Braille, the young boy could only see light, shadow and indistinct shapes. But, at the age of seventeen, Meir Schneider went to work learning The Bates Method, spending up to 13 hours each and every day practicing countless eye exercises and focusing on improving his "emotional outlook."

Guess what? The Bates Method worked!

Over time, his vision improved dramatically. And today Dr. Meir Schneider is currently licensed to drive a car without the use of corrective eyeglasses or contact lenses. Incredible!

The fact is, the invaluable information and thought-provoking insight gained from people like Dr. Hatsopolous, Dr. Bates, and Dr. Schneider, and particularly from the many case studies on Dissociative Identity Disorder like Barb's, helps all of us realize the mind does, in fact, have no limitations.

But the most exciting part in this discussion about the amazing power of the human mind, and what keeps me thrilled about the future, is there's so much more to discover.

CHAPTER 5

THE CONSCIOUS MIND

Any discussion about the factors that create success starts with the conscious mind because it is the part of the brain most familiar to us. The conscious mind is that part of your brain you hear "talking" inside your head all day long. It's your "thinking mind," the mind you know and are always "aware" of.

Have you ever heard a conversation in your head that sounds like this . . .

"I should take out the garbage. Jeez,
it's heavy . . . what did I put in there?
. . . boy, the grass is getting long . . .
looks like the mail has come already
. . . I'll grab the mail on my way back . . .
bills, bills . . . blecchh! . . . it was so stupid
to buy that big screen TV! . . . stupid . . .
stupid . . . stupid . . . oh, look, it's the furniture
outlet flyer . . . wow, a 50% off sale! . . .
jeez, I gotta mow this lawn . . . my back
hurts . . . I wonder what I did to it . . . I should
really mow this lawn . . . but it would probably
be bad for my back . . . I'm so tired . . . Maybe I'll
mow later."

. . . and on, and on . . . and on.

I think you get the idea. Your conscious mind—your thinking mind—is all of that inner chatter you hear in your head all day long. It's always running in the background, giving you play-by-play and color commentary like a mini-sportscaster.

If you listen closely to this mini-sportscaster and its commentary, you'll see much of the time it's merely describing whatever is in front of you, all the mundane, everyday stuff of your life.

I don't know about you, but I sometimes think this mini-sportscaster in my mind would look like some wacky, zany, chatterbox of a woman . . . always talking.

However, it's probably worth noting that sometimes the commentary in my head is not positive and you may experience this too.

Do you remember the old cartoons where there was a recurring female character who always carried a rolling pin and was always ready to whack someone? Sometimes it feels like the commentator in my head is really critical and waiting to hit me over the head with a rolling pin, like that classic cartoon woman.

In addition to being the sportscaster of your day-to-day life, the conscious mind actually performs some quite useful functions.

The conscious mind is the part of the brain you use when you want to recall information from your past, such as a fond memory or someone's name . . . or maybe where you parked your car.

It's also useful when you are planning your future, goal setting, visioning, creating, or using your imagination.

The conscious mind is also the part of your brain helping you make decisions, focus your attention, and complete tasks.

When you are faced with a task that is new, like learning a brand new computer program or a task that is extremely difficult, such as writing an essay or a complicated mathematical problem, you use your conscious mind to focus and accomplish the task.

This is a really important point, which we will revisit in the next section, but for now, think of it this way . . . when you come into this world, you are a clean slate. You have to "learn" everything.

Physical acts like standing, walking, or picking up objects, you actually had to learn how to do these things at one time and when you did, it took your full conscious attention.

Think about a toddler learning to stand. He or she is using his or her full conscious concentration to learn such an amazing skill. The same was true for you when you were learning to stand, walk, or pick up objects.

Simply put, the conscious mind is your thinking mind. It's the part of your brain you understand, know, and are most aware of. I'm sure you've heard René DesCartes' famous philosophical statement, "I think, therefore, I am."—which basically means, you exist because of your thoughts.

This may be true, but the statement only tells half the story.

It's easy for us to get attached to our conscious mind and mistakenly think this is who we are, but as you'll learn in this book, your thoughts are merely tools for building a "truer picture" of yourself, a picture of who you want to be.

CHAPTER 6

THE UNCONSCIOUS MIND

If the conscious mind is most familiar to you, then the unconscious mind is the part of your brain you're probably not so familiar with and not quite sure how it works.

The unconscious mind is sometimes referred to as the subconscious mind. I prefer the term "unconscious" for a variety of reasons. First, the word subconscious is not a recognized psychological term. It's not recognized at all by the psychology community.

Next, I believe the preface "sub" implies it is subordinate or less-than other parts of the brain, and nothing could be further from the truth.

Finally, I think the term unconscious has less "cultural baggage" than the term subconscious. Hollywood has exploited the idea we all have these deep, impure thoughts lurking in our subconscious just waiting to surface at any moment . . . or a favorite in today's personal development circles . . . deep-seeded thoughts, waiting to "sabotage" our success.

Again, nothing could be further from the truth. The unconscious mind is much more beneficial to you than you've probably been led to believe.

For starters, unconscious mind is the part of your brain regulating all of your bodily functions. It's responsible for making sure your heart beats, your blood flows, and that you breathe normally.

Imagine for a second what your life would be like if you had to consciously remember to breathe each moment. Imagine putting this on your list of things to do: buy bread, take the dog out for a walk . . . oh, yeah . . . breathe! Somehow I don't think that would be a very successful system!

The point is, you don't forget to breathe and you don't need to put it on a list of things to do, because the "decision" to breathe is made unconsciously by you.

In other words, everything you take for granted regarding your body, the things you depend on for survival—digesting your food, processing food into energy, sweating, your beating heart, your flowing blood, and breathing—the unconscious mind takes care of for you.

In addition, this truly essential part of your brain executes all the functions of the body you've learned so well and so completely they've literally become "unconscious" to you.

Remember in the last chapter when I said that we use the conscious mind to focus and learn? Remember the toddler learning to stand? He or she is using their full conscious concentration to learn such an amazing skill. The same was true for you when you were learning to stand, walk, or pick up objects.

Over time, you then became so proficient at standing, walking, and picking up things, there wasn't much need for you to include these acts in your "conscious awareness" anymore. Your unconscious mind now performs these tasks for you. You now accomplish these tasks seemingly without thinking about them.

Think about all of the intricate movements that are involved in picking up an object or walking across a room. You no longer have to "think" about all of the tiny details in order to perform these daily skills.

Many of your daily repetitious activities are performed by your unconscious mind . . . activities like combing your hair, brushing your teeth, showering, doing the dishes, taking out the garbage, and even driving your car!

Have you ever had that experience? The experience of driving your car and then suddenly realizing you've driven the last 20 miles without even being "aware" of it?

Most of us take these types of unconscious actions for granted. While our conscious mind is busy thinking about more important things, our unconscious mind is doing all the "mundane work" for us, performing many of our day-to-day tasks.

Some experts estimate that 95% of our daily waking time is spent doing unconscious acts! Can you imagine that?

Now let me add another layer onto that . . . the unconscious mind is also where you record all the information about your identity. I like to compare this part of the brain to an old "tape recorder," recording your memories, your thoughts and ideas, and even your character traits.

Think about it. We all have certain ideas about ourselves. You don't need a checklist to "remember" certain traits about yourself. You could be . . . quick to temper . . . not artistic . . . a chocolate lover . . . a poor swimmer . . . an animal lover . . . shy in crowds . . . or . . . not a morning person.

The reason you don't need a checklist is because you've kept running these "tapes" inside your head, telling yourself over and over again, that you are, in fact, quick to temper or shy in crowds or a lover of animals, so you don't really need to "think" about these things consciously anymore.

You learned these ideas about yourself in the same way you learned how to stand, walk, or pick up objects. You practiced them over and over again until you turned them over to the unconscious mind. After you store these ideas about yourself and the world around you in the unconscious mind, they are called "beliefs."

You came to an "agreement" with these thoughts about yourself, and your agreement solidifies these thoughts into your unconscious mind, essentially making up who you "believe" you are.

I'll get into more detail about beliefs in future chapters, but the important thing to remember is that when you have a belief formed in your unconscious mind, you act on it automatically, without "thinking" about it, just like you walk across a room or pick up an object without "thinking" about it.

The unconscious mind's ability to regulate so much of our day-to-day existence is truly incredible. As you'll learn in future chapters, when we learn how to change the beliefs stored in the unconscious mind, change in our lives truly becomes effortless.

CHAPTER 7

BELIEFS

Now that you have a more clear understanding of the difference between the conscious and unconscious mind, I'd like to tell you a little bit more about how beliefs are formed.

As we said in the last chapter, what we repeatedly think about ultimately solidifies in the unconscious mind as a belief. And, as you'll learn, beliefs are pretty powerful things. So let's talk about them.

If you ask people how beliefs are formed in the unconscious, most people will say parents or siblings influence some beliefs; others might come from friends, while others come from the culture in which we're raised.

Many experts agree beliefs are formed during early childhood years, most before the age of six. We spend much of our first years of life learning all the "rules" of our culture, mostly accepting these rules without question. In essence, we don't have much choice or input on beliefs formed before age six.

But something happens to all of us after the age of six. We start forming our own beliefs. We develop a more discerning eye of the world. We compare ourselves to others and we make judgments. And our beliefs are then formed by either "agreeing or disagreeing" with what we see and hear around us. In other words—after the age of six—we have a clear "choice" to make regarding what we see and hear and whether we "refuse" or "give consent" to these things.

Here is an example of what I mean by giving consent:

Imagine a boy in an art class drawing a picture. Sitting next to him is a little girl who draws a picture that gets the teacher's attention, and many of the classmates' attention. Everyone tells the little girl her picture is fantastic. Yet little or no attention is given to the boy's drawing. Naturally, thinking his drawing is not as good as the girl's, the boy thinks, "I'm no good at art, but she is."

Can we really blame the boy for having this thought? Probably not . . . yet, no one has told the boy he isn't good at art.

So how has he come to this conclusion about himself?

Well, the boy probably looked around the classroom, took notice of all the acclaim given to the girl's drawing by the teacher and his classmates, and also noticed the lack of praise or attention given to his own drawing. And, subsequently, the world around him became the only evidence he needed to form a belief about his drawing ability

Despite the evidence, the boy still has a choice to make. Remember, no one has actually informed him he isn't good at art; he has come up with this conscious thought all by himself. Many of us would probably do the same.

The more important point here is whether the boy agrees or disagrees with this thought. Will he keep running the same tape in his head, "I'm no good at art"? Will he keep giving his consent? And, ultimately, will this be the belief "formed" in the boy's unconscious mind? Will the boy truly "believe" he is no good at art?

Before a conscious thought is formed in your unconscious mind, you still have a choice to agree or disagree with this thought. This one crucial choice will determine whether you form a negative or positive belief in your mind. The point is, you always have a choice.

You also have a choice to agree or disagree with a thought even after it's been formed into your unconscious.

I'll discuss this more in depth as it applies to your business later in this book.

It's funny. I always remember having this feeling of a dark and disturbing section of my brain called the "subconscious mind" where all sorts of horrible thoughts supposedly lurked, and that I basically had no control over what was stored inside my head.

I finally came to realize this was a myth.

I have learned my own beliefs are just an accumulation of my own, day-to-day "conscious agreement" with the world around me . . . my own day-to-day conscious thoughts. I have realized I always have a choice about what kinds of beliefs get stored inside my head.

This was such an exciting time for me as I realized this: I could just as easily form positive beliefs in my unconscious as I could negative beliefs.

So it doesn't really matter whether you have a positive or negative thought in your head. You still have to continue giving consent to this thought for it to remain in your unconscious mind as a belief.

Think of this in your business. If you have old tapes running in your head telling you, "I'm not good at managing people" or "I can't learn new things" or "I'm not good at managing my time" or "I'm no good at talking to people . . . remember this one important thing about old tapes or beliefs . . .

IF YOU CAN AGREE WITH A THOUGHT,

YOU CAN ALSO <u>DISAGREE</u> WITH THE SAME THOUGHT!

Remember the young boy's thought, "I'm no good at art"? Didn't you see how easily one thought could become formed in the boy's unconscious as a belief with just one simple agreement, even though no one ever told him he wasn't good at art?

I say "could" become formed as a belief here, because I wanted to leave the boy's story open-ended, to show that it doesn't take much to go from a "simple conscious thought" to a belief, and that all your beliefs—whether they are positive or negative—are solely determined by the choices you make about your thoughts.

You'll learn from conducting your Mindware Experiments, "conscious positive thoughts" will become powerful building blocks to create your own personal and financial success because these thoughts will form in your unconscious mind as new beliefs. And these new, powerful modes of thought last longer, they never let you down, and you never have to run old negative tapes about yourself again.

And you'll also see your old beliefs—no matter how long they've been stored inside you—are "changeable" and erased as easily as they are made.

Old negative beliefs can easily be removed and replaced.

And when old beliefs are replaced, they're history.

You will never go back to those old beliefs about yourself ever again.

••

Simply put, beliefs are both powerful ***and*** changeable.

••

And as you continue this book, you'll learn how to change your beliefs and harness the full power of your unconscious mind.

CHAPTER 8

OUR BEST FRIEND, THE UNCONSCIOUS MIND

By now I think you're getting a clear picture of how beliefs are formed in the unconscious mind. In order to change those beliefs, I'd like to reveal a few other characteristics of the unconscious mind that will be useful for creating change.

For starters, the unconscious mind is like your "best friend" because it supports every single thought you have, loves you dearly, and it never passes judgment on you. However, it's a best friend with no sense of humor. It takes every thought you have literally. Think of Mr. Spock from Star Trek here.

For example, if your thought is, "I'm no good at art," your unconscious mind, like a supportive best friend will say to you, "Yes. You're right. You're no good at art."

If you think to yourself, "I want a lot of clients for my business," your unconscious mind says "Yes. You should have a lot of clients."

If you follow that up with the thought, "That would be a lot of hard work," your unconscious mind pipes in, saying, "Yes. That would be hard work."

If you say, "I can really see myself losing some weight," the unconscious mind supporting you through thick and thin, will say, "Yes, I can see you losing weight, too."

BUT if you follow that thought with another thought such as, "but I always seem to gain it back," the unconscious mind again says, "Yes, you always gain it back."

If you say to yourself, "I'm such an idiot. I locked my keys in the car," your unconscious mind will say to you, "Yes, you are an idiot."

I'm sure you're getting the point. Every single thought you have, the unconscious mind will support without question, because the unconscious mind doesn't discriminate between your thoughts.

So the bad news is . . . every thought you have has the potential to become a belief.

And the good news is . . . every thought you have has the potential to become a belief.

So in lieu of this information, it's easy to stop "fearing" your unconscious mind. There is no need to worry about all the ways in which it might seem to be controlling your life or preventing you from getting what you desire. Conducting your Mindware Experiments will help you train your brain to see the unconscious mind as something you influence easily.

CHAPTER 9

IS IT REAL OR IMAGINED?

There is one final point I'd like to make about the unconscious mind and it may be the most important one so far. So important that I thought it needed an entire chapter of it's own and so here it is . . .

The unconscious mind doesn't know the difference between what is "real" and what is "imagined."

Remember from the previous section, the unconscious mind doesn't discriminate between your thoughts. This holds true whether you are having a thought in reaction to the "real" world around you or whether you are having a thought about something "imagined" or fabricated in your head.

For example, if you imagine you're playing hockey, your unconscious mind is "storing the experience" of playing hockey, as though it's actually happening. If you imagine the feel of the skates on your feet, the cold wind on your face, and the sense of balance it takes to stand upright, your unconscious mind believes you are actually playing hockey.

To the unconscious mind, it doesn't really matter whether you are literally playing hockey, or imagining you are playing hockey. Remember, the unconscious mind doesn't discriminate between what is real and what is imagined.

But, really, how can we be certain this is true?

Well, professional athletes have used methods of visualization and "mental rehearsal" for years to perfect their games. In fact, when researchers hook up an athlete to a biofeedback machine, the athlete's muscles will literally "fire" or register on the feedback machine as though they are actually performing their routine, even though the athlete is only thinking about these physical acts.

An actual study done by Dr. Judd Blasotto at the University of Chicago, attempted to determine the effects of visualization on the performance of athletes shooting a basketball. Dr. Blasotto's findings showed that physical performance was enhanced by the repetition of certain physical acts, but it was also enhanced through visualization or "rehearsing" these acts in the mind.

Dr. Blasotto wanted to measure basketball players' percentage of successful free throws vs. total shots taken. He randomly sorted players into three groups. At the beginning of the study, all three groups were tested for their ability to successfully make shots from the free throw line. Each person in each group was informed they'd be coming back in one month and tested again.

The first group was told to do absolutely nothing for a month. Just forget about basketball for the next month. Do zilch, nada, nothing. The second group was told to hit the courts every day for a month and do at least one-hour of free-throw practice. Finally, like the first group, the third group was told to refrain from doing anything physical but, instead, to spend an hour each day "visualizing" shooting successful free throws.

Thirty days later, when each athlete was tested again, the first group (who did nothing during the one month) didn't show any improvement whatsoever, which isn't too surprising. The second group (who physically shot free throws every day) showed a performance increase of 24%. And the third group (who didn't actually pick up a basketball for 30 days but, instead, visualized shooting successful free throws every day) showed a performance increase of 23%!

Let me repeat that. The third group didn't pick up a basketball for 30 days and still nearly matched the efforts of the group who practiced shooting free throws every day for one hour. Amazing!

The University of Chicago's study literally revolutionized the way athletes look at themselves on their performance and how adding visualization to a training regimen can dramatically improve physical performance.

Again, the mind just doesn't know the difference between what's real and what's imagined.

But don't take my word for it. Let's test this theory of visualization with a little experiment. Read through this exercise first, and then follow through on your own.

Let's begin . . .

Close your eyes. Imagine you are standing in your kitchen. Imagine yourself as though you are "in your body." In other words, use your "mind's eye." Even though your eyes are closed, imagine the room as though you are looking through your own eyes. Visualize.

Now, with your eyes closed, using your mind's eye, imagine everything around you as you stand in the middle of the kitchen. Maybe it's the temperature in the room or the hum of the refrigerator. Just take in all the different sounds, smells, and sights around you.

Visualize walking up to your refrigerator and opening the door. Feel the blast of cold air escaping from the refrigerator and notice there is a small lemon sitting on the center of the top shelf. Imagine reaching out and picking up the lemon and noticing how cold and firm it is when you touch it. You can feel the small pockmarks on the rind—it is heavy and firm with juice.

With eyes still closed, imagine yourself holding the lemon in your hand, shutting the refrigerator door and walking over to your kitchen counter. Place the lemon on a cutting board in front of you. See yourself picking up a knife sitting next to the cutting board and slicing through the center of the lemon, cutting it in half. The knife is very sharp and it slices through the lemon easily. Notice the juice oozing out of the lemon and onto the cutting board.

Now visualize picking up half of the lemon and placing the juicy side into your mouth and biting down. You salivate from the taste.

Okay, open your eyes. Did you salivate at the thought of biting into that lemon? Most people do. Why? The reason a person salivates just from a description or visualization of biting into a lemon is because the mind isn't distinguishing between what's real and what's imagined. The mind, actually "believing" it's biting into a real lemon, functions as it normally would, causing you to salivate.

This is the power of the mind. And this is why people talk about foods they love with the expression, "I can almost taste it," or "It makes my mouth water."

Again, the mind can't differentiate between the real and the imagined.

Everyone uses visualization in some form on a daily basis. If you are one of those who say, "I can't visualize" and you actually salivated when you imagined biting into the lemon, visualization is exactly what you did. Every time you leave your seat in a restaurant, go to the bathroom and find your way back to your seat, you are using visualization to "map out" your way back. Or think about when you may have remembered where you parked in a large parking lot. Visualization is how you found your car.

We also use visualization when we reminisce about times gone by or anytime we recall a memory from the past . . . a camping trip, a softball game, an old job, or your childhood house. In all of these instances, you are using visualization.

Now that you have a better understanding of how the conscious and unconscious mind work and how beliefs are formed in the unconscious mind, in the next chapter we'll be discussing our own personal filtering system, which supports our beliefs and our own personal picture of the world.

CHAPTER 10

THE RETICULAR ACTIVATING SYSTEM

It's difficult to fathom the amount of information our unconscious mind processes for us. We literally have BILLIONS of bits of information coming at us every day. Think about the colors, sounds, and sensations that are coming at us in every second of every day.

In fact, the conscious mind, which processes information at a rate of about 40 bits per second, PALES in comparison to the work of the unconscious mind, which processes information at a rate of 40 million bits per second! Wow, huh?

Obviously, it would be impossible to sort through everything we see, hear, touch, taste, smell, and feel each and every moment of each and every day. We need something that prevents us from overloading . . . something that keeps us sane. Luckily, there is a part of our brain located between the conscious mind and unconscious mind that "filters out" much of this information.

This small filter is called the Reticular Activating System, and it helps to keep us sane by looking for information in the outside world that "matches" the beliefs already stored in the unconscious mind.

In other words, this filter in our brains—the Reticular Activating System—acts like a tireless little matchmaker, always making sure our outside world picture matches our inside world picture.

Here's what I mean by our outside world picture and our inside world picture. As we're forming beliefs about ourselves, about other people, and about the world around us, our mind is taking in a lot of contradictory information, both positive and negative. And as we learned earlier, how we respond to this information with our own thoughts and emotions essentially creates our belief system, and this belief system makes up our inside picture of the world.

Let's go back to our boy in the art class, to see how inside world pictures are formed.

Remember, one day he saw the little girl next to him as a good artist and himself as, well, not so good.

As the story continues, we find the boy making chalk drawings on the sidewalk with his neighborhood friends. At the end of the day, the boy compares his own drawings to the ones by his friends, and thinks to himself that his own drawings are pretty darn good.

The following week, the boy visits his aunt and cousin, and they go to the lake and build sand castles on the beach as part of a children's art contest. The boy's castle comes in fourth place. His cousin, two years older, places seventh. This doesn't elicit much of a response in the boy. He thinks coming in fourth place is not so bad. But, thinking again, the boy wonders whether coming in fourth place is any good at all.

A couple days later, back in art class, the boy paints a picture of a tiger. He feels pretty good about his painting but when the art teacher remarks to him, "Good job. Is that a bobcat?" The boy immediately thinks his painting's not so good because he was, after all, trying to paint a tiger.

As you can see, the boy's "conscious thoughts" about his artistic ability run the gamut as he continues gathering evidence from the world around him.

Each situation has elicited a different response from him and it's really up in the air which belief will eventually be formed in the boy's unconscious mind.

But at some point, after he's gathered enough evidence, he will form a belief about his artistic ability. This belief will be based on which conscious thoughts make it into the unconscious mind and which thoughts get filtered out. It is also dependent on what choices the boy makes about all the different information coming into his awareness.

It's important to note that even though experts know very little about how conscious thoughts themselves are formed. Why do we have thoughts? We know plenty about what causes some conscious thoughts to be filtered out while others make it into the unconscious mind.

So what makes it through the filter? Well, typically, more "emotionally charged" conscious thoughts weigh more "heavily in the mind" and therefore tend to make it through the filter, making much more likely for them to end up in the unconscious mind as formed beliefs.

Let's go back to the boy again. If his more negative conscious thoughts about his drawings in the class are more "emotionally charged" for him than placing fourth in a sandcastle contest, or his feelings about his sidewalk drawings, then those thoughts with more emotional impact will have a much greater likelihood of making it through and forming a belief for him.

And when this belief is formed, the boy's unconscious mind will then support the belief that he isn't a good artist by filtering out any and all information that doesn't "match" this internal world picture. The boy's internal world picture—in the form of a belief which says, "I am not a good artist"—will always find a match with the boy's outside world picture. This is how the mind works.

More importantly, even though there may be evidence in his future indicating, in fact, that the boy does have some artistic talents, he will develop a "blind spot" to this evidence. Once again, the filter in our brains, the Reticular Activating System, literally prevents positive evidence from coming into the boy's awareness. From now on, the boy will only "see" evidence that points to his lack of artistic ability. Why?

Remember, the boy's inner world picture—his personal belief that he isn't a good artist—must find a match with his outer world picture. And as more and more matches are made between the boy's inside and outside pictures of the world, the belief becomes stronger and stronger, and any information contrary to this belief doesn't even exist for the boy. He is blind to it. He isn't good at art, and there's no other way to look at it.

Again, with billions of bits of information coming at us every minute, the filter in our brains, the Reticular Activating System, helps us "manage" all the bits of external stimuli coming into our heads, and it also ensures the only information allowed in already matches those beliefs formed in our unconscious mind.

And so remember . . . ***the outside world picture will always match the inside world picture***.

CHAPTER 11

THE RETICULAR ACTIVATING SYSTEM IN ACTION

Now let's see some examples of the Reticular Activating System in action. Let me give an example of how it works in business. Here's a story of how a blind spot might affect someone's business and this is a true story of someone I worked with . . .

Her name is Joyce. Joyce came to me because her business wasn't growing and she wanted help. I asked Joyce about why she thought her business wasn't growing and she said that lived in a small town and she said that the people in her town either didn't have money or they were cheap and so she wasn't selling her products and services.

After further talking with Joyce, I discovered that in reality, her business started out like many small business owners . . . she started out feeling quite enthusiastic. She was excited and exuded the same "ignorance on fire" beginnings of so many of us and initially she saw some real successes . . .

. . . but then she hit a bump in the road . . . or two. She had a few rejections, had a few minor setbacks and, after these few bumps in the road . . . she had a few customers tell her that they couldn't afford her products. A few customers told her that money was tight and that her products and services weren't in their budgets. And surprisingly quickly, even after the first customer or two, she heard this little voice in her head saying things like . . . "These people have no money to spend" . . . and . . . "Nobody in this town can afford my products and services."

It wasn't a loud voice . . . it was just a little gnawing voice telling her that the people in her town were either broke or cheap . . . and it was a gnawing little voice that just kept getting louder and more annoying.

Prior to coming to me, she had tried some other techniques regarding bringing her business online, but she wasn't having any success with these techniques. By the time she got on the phone with me, you could cut her frustration with a knife. She was not only frustrated with her business . . . she was actually feeling animosity towards the people in her town . . . the people she ultimately wanted to be her customers . . . and needless to say, the growth of her business had completely stalled.

She had a belief in her unconscious mind (her inside picture of the world) that said, "people cannot afford my products and services"

After that belief is formed in the unconscious mind, the Reticular Activating System starts doing it's work on her behalf—and any information contrary to this belief was never allowed into her awareness.

Because contrary information was never allowed in, the belief remained intact, ensuring that Joyce would remain "blind" to anything around her that might change her belief.

And even though it's common knowledge that in every town, every state, and every nation, there are people who are open with their money, people who are frugal, people who are conservative with their money, people who are liberal, people who are rich, and people who are poor—Joyce couldn't "see" this as part of her outside world picture—because of the "blind spot" was created by the Reticular Activating System. It was filtering out that information. It's almost as if this kind of world didn't "exist" for Joyce. Unfortunately, her Reticular Activating System was only "honing in" on those people with limited financial means.

Her internal picture of the world was that "most people can't afford my product," and her unconscious mind immediately sorted through all the people she came into contact with, making sure she only "noticed" people matching this description. She would only over-hear conversations from people who were having a hard time making ends meet.

In other words, after we've formed beliefs in our unconscious mind and created an inside picture of the world based on these beliefs, it doesn't matter what the outside world around us is "saying."

The bottom line and this is very important . . . The Reticular Activating System, the filter in your brain has one full-time job . . . it spends all day every day matching your outside picture of the world with your inside picture of the world. Whatever you believe on the inside will show up again and again in your outside world.

The good news is that the Mindware Experiments you'll be taking part in with Train Your Brain will help you remove your blind spots. And, then, your Reticular Activating System, the filter in your brains, can go to work for you by allowing "new information" into your awareness. This is exactly how it worked for Joyce and it will work for you too.

Before we leave this segment on beliefs, I want to make one final point about the unconscious mind.

The unconscious mind makes sure we "act" within the parameters of our beliefs. This means that during a normal 24-hour day, 95% of the time we are acting unconsciously based on beliefs stored in our unconscious mind.

Therefore, you don't have to flip through a list of character traits before you react in any given situation . . . "Am I outgoing? Am I a good listener? Am I a jokester? Am I too serious? Am I good with kids? Am I serious about work? Am I a downer? Am I moody? Am I shy? Am I an optimist?"

You never need to think about "who you are" or what you "believe" because the unconscious mind takes care of all that for you, without question or judgment.

In other words, if you believe you are painfully shy and you walk into a room full of people you don't know, you don't have a conscious thought about how this makes you feel.

If the belief you hold is that you are extremely shy, your unconscious mind immediately tells your body to constrict breathing, tells your heart to beat faster, and tells your palms to sweat. Your body reacts without having one single conscious thought about being shy, because your unconscious mind knows full well who you are and how you will react to a room full of people you've met for the first time.

The unconscious mind, your tried-and-true friend, will make sure you act "like yourself" automatically. Just like you walk across a room or pick up an object "without thinking" about it, you will always act "like yourself" without thinking about it too.

The conscious mind, your "thinking mind," will set goals and perform many tasks for you. But remember, it's the unconscious mind that is sorting through those 40 million bits of information per second and bringing into your awareness only those things matching your inside picture of the world. This means 95% of the time, the unconscious mind running the show.

CHAPTER 12

THOUGHT PRECEDES EMOTION

I really want to drive home the idea that how you "see" the world around you is always determined by your thoughts. What do I mean by this?

Well, let's say six people attend a business seminar. All six are in the same room and listening to the same person give the same presentation.

Even though on the surface everything seems the same for each person, each person's "experience"—their thoughts and emotions—will differ greatly. Why?

Because thoughts not only form beliefs, they also generate emotion.

So if you pay special attention to the corresponding emotion each person feels as he or she sits through this presentation, you will see six very different interpretations based on the same information.

The first attendee's thought is . . . "This is so great. I've never heard any of this before and I can't wait to apply this to my business!" Corresponding emotion is excitement.

The second attendee's thought is . . . "This is a lot of the same stuff I've heard before, but maybe I'll pay attention and maybe I'll find a new nugget I haven't heard before." Corresponding emotion is positive expectation or anticipation.

The third attendee's thought is . . . "This is the same old, same old. I know all this stuff already. What a waste of my time." Corresponding emotion is boredom or frustration.

The fourth attendee's thought is . . . "I don't think I can do this business. I wonder if I should just throw in the towel. She seems so good. I could never be like her." Corresponding emotion is fear or worry.

The fifth attendee's thought is, "I can't believe my boyfriend is really serious about breaking up. I love him so much. I wonder if I should call him. What will I do without him?" Corresponding emotion is sadness.

The sixth attendee's thought is, "She's making some really good points here. This sounds really do-able. I know I can get the hang of this. She makes the steps sound really easy." Corresponding emotion is assuredness or knowing.

So there it is. It's the same room, same fluorescent lights, same presentation, same presenter, but six different thought responses, as well as six different corresponding emotional responses. There are as many responses as there are people in the room. Why?

Well, let's take a closer look. Notice some attendees are having a pleasant experience and some, not so pleasant. Some have positive feelings about the seminar and some have negative feelings. One attendee even has thoughts about her boyfriend, which doesn't really relate to the seminar at all. So what causes each person to have different responses to the seminar they're attending?

One word . . . thoughts.

As I said previously, thoughts perform the important task of helping you form beliefs in your unconscious mind. But that's not all that thoughts do for you. They actually perform another equally important function . . .

· ·

Thoughts "generate" <u>all</u> of your emotions.

In other words, your feelings in any situation are always preceded by your thoughts, and it's these thoughts that cause you to "experience" a particular emotion.

· ·

I'm sure you've heard the expressions, "My emotions got the best of me" . . . or . . . "I couldn't control my emotions."

These age-old expressions suggest we have little or no control over our feelings. Well, I want to say one thing right now . . . nothing is further from the truth.

Emotion isn't a random thing invading your body or taking over your mind. There's a good logical reason for feeling the way you do. And even though you may feel you're being held captive by your emotion— whether you're feeling overwhelmed, overstressed or overworked—your own thoughts are generating or "creating" this emotion for you.

Needless to say, thoughts accomplish many important things for you. Thoughts help you form beliefs. They help you form your inside picture of the world, which then forms your outside pictures of the world. Your perception or how you "look" at the world is influenced by your thoughts.

Most importantly, thoughts generate all of your emotions.

Very soon, you'll conduct your first Mindware Experiment and you'll experience first hand the power of your thoughts to create your emotions. As you continue this book, you'll understand more and more just how important thought and emotion are in creating your own success.

Ultimately, your moment-to-moment experiences can be happy, fun, nice, pleasant, unpleasant, frustrating, irritating, or infuriating. But there is nothing random about the way you feel. And whether you are feeling joyous or angry, that particular emotion is always preceded by a particular (joyous or angry) thought in your head.

Always.

CHAPTER 13

EMOTIONAL PRIMER

By now you've got a pretty good handle on the conscious mind and the unconscious mind—and the roles that beliefs and thoughts play. Next, I'd like to talk a little bit about emotion.

When creating your inside picture of the world, emotion serves two important roles for you.

First, as we mentioned earlier, emotionally charged conscious thoughts, or those weighing heavily in your mind, make it through the filter in your brain and typically end up in the unconscious mind as beliefs.

If you can look at your thoughts as the crucial building blocks needed to form beliefs in the unconscious mind, then you can also look at any emotion attached to these thoughts as the glue solidifying your thoughts into your brain.

The second and more important role emotion plays for you is as an emotional "barometer." What do I mean by this? Well, emotion will help you gauge if you're moving toward or away from achieving your goals, whatever they may be.

In other words, whether the positive dreams you've been visualizing for yourself and your business are coming "true" for you. How you feel is your "barometer." If you feel good, those dreams are on the way and if you feel negative, you are blocking those dreams from coming to you.

Let me explain. What we know about the close link between thought and emotion we know in "forward motion"—which is to say thought "creates" emotion.

But when you look at this link in reverse, you first "gauge" how you're feeling at a particular time or what emotion you're experiencing, you can use it as a clear indicator of the thoughts you are thinking.

How are you feeling about your business as it relates to your sales, client relations, growth, cash flow, or any other aspect of your business? Are you completely stressed out? Are you overwhelmed? Are you feeling a sense of helplessness or hopelessness? Or are you excited? Are you feeling hopeful? Are you filled with anticipation of the good things coming your way? Feeling positive? Whatever emotion you're experiencing, "How you feel" is a clear indicator of the types of thoughts you're having about your business. Remember, what you're "feeling" always reflects what you're "thinking."

In these types of situations, thought and emotion are so closely linked sometimes it's hard to distinguish between the two, and you often end up feeling as though you can't "control" your emotion. That's why it's important for you to separate the two, by first getting a good assessment of your emotions—"How do I feel?"—then take a good look at what kinds of thoughts preceded these feelings.

When the "close link" between thought and emotion becomes clear to you and how they both directly affect your business, you will be able to" use" thought and emotion to your advantage in your business. How?

Well, in the same way you want to pay attention to "negative feelings"—which you'll quickly learn are always the result of some kind of counterproductive thought—your Mindware Experiments will also show you that constructive or affirmative thinking will always create a positive emotion for you.

And, as a result, by consistently incorporating this knowledge about yourself into your daily life, you will remove those unwanted and seemingly immovable obstacles to success. And you will create more resourceful mind and that in turn will create "noticeable positive shifts" in your business.

Our first Mindware Experiment further illustrates the direct connection between thought and emotion and how you can use this close relationship to your advantage in your business.

You may continue reading or go to part two of this book and play with Mindware Experiment #1—Thoughts Control Feelings and Mindware Experiment #2—Staying Aware: What Thoughts Am I Thinking Right Now?

CHAPTER 14

THE CYCLE OF
PERPETUAL SAMENESS

In this chapter, I'd like to put all the pieces we've discussed in the previous chapters together and explain The Cycle of Perpetual Sameness.

In order to explain The Cycle of Perpetual Sameness, I'd like to start by taking a look at the effects of repetition in the unconscious mind as it relates to beliefs.

Let's start with a belief already stored in your unconscious mind. Let's say, for example, you know yourself as the type of person who procrastinates and you miss deadlines because of it.

Unconscious Mind
(beliefs)
Inside World Picture

You might have noticed that I used the word "know." I said you "know" yourself as the type of person who procrastinates. I used this word because that's how it feels when you have a strong belief about yourself. You don't question it. You may feel it has almost become a "fact" for you. Why?

Because when you "give your consent" to a belief over and over again, the belief itself gets stronger and stronger, and develops in the unconscious mind as though it's factual or truthful. It's beyond belief. There's no questioning it! Procrastinate? "What can I say? I know I'll procrastinate. It's me. It's who I am."

And so you do procrastinate.

And what really makes a belief stronger?

One word: repetition.

Remember, conscious thoughts "pumped-up with emotion" make their way through the filter ending up as beliefs stored in the unconscious mind.

Well, repetition plays an equally important role in forming your beliefs.

When you "give consent" to a belief over and over again, this belief becomes so much a part of your being you wouldn't think of questioning it. You don't need to. Good or bad, it's just who you are.

And that's why in almost every instance in your life you're typically acting in accordance with those beliefs stored in your unconscious mind. You're always acting "in character."

Remember your unconscious mind is your best friend. It's always trying to "lighten the load" for you by remembering how to do all of those thing you learned so well, whether those things are actions like walking or picking up objects or whether they are your own character traits.

So there is never any need on your part to try to figure out which character traits make up your personality. And there's also no need for you to "take inventory" of which beliefs are stored inside your brain.

The unconscious mind keeps track of these for you automatically, ensuring you act accordingly at all times. Again, because you've given consent to these aspects of your personality through repetition, you don't have to think about how to act. In essence, you've given your unconscious mind carte blanche to do for you as it sees fit. In fact, much of what you think about, how you feel, or what you believe, is done unconsciously. As we learned, we're acting unconsciously 95% of the time.

Unfortunately, this can be a double-edged sword. Sure, it's great that the unconscious mind manages things in your busy little head, but this can be troublesome when your beliefs keep you on The Cycle of Perpetual Sameness.

Remember, one of the most important tasks the unconscious mind performs for you is making sure your outside world picture (the world around you) matches your inside world picture (those beliefs firmly planted inside your head).

So when you have a belief stored in the unconscious mind, like for example that you are the type of person who procrastinates. Then when the opportunity arises to procrastinate, you will do it.

Outside World Picture
(behaviour, outcomes, and
the world around us.)

Unconscious Mind
(beliefs)
Inside World Picture

And it doesn't matter if the world around you is telling you that hitting deadlines is important in the business world, or that procrastinating might hurt your chance for success. Your Reticular Activating System will make sure to focus your attention on other things besides the most important task at hand. It helps your brain to rationalize that you have plenty of time and next thing you know, you look at the calendar and you're under a deadline and you're flipping out because you know you usually meet deadlines.

Again, your outside world picture (the world around you) matches your inside picture of the world (those beliefs firmly planted inside your head).

So how does it turn into a Cycle of Perpetual Sameness?

Well, if you just procrastinated, didn't worry about it and went about your day, there probably wouldn't be any cycle, but that's not usually how it works, is it?

Often after you procrastinate, you start with a barrage of insults in your mind. The rolling pin comes out and the negative self-talk kicks in and it sounds something like this . . .

> "Dang it, I procrastinated again."
> "What is my problem?"
> "I'm such a loser."
> "Now I'm late and I'll have to rush. I hate that."
> "I'm such an idiot."
> "It's no wonder I can't get anything done."
> "Why can't I ever hit a deadline?"
> "'I'll never make it in time."

. . . And so on, and so on.

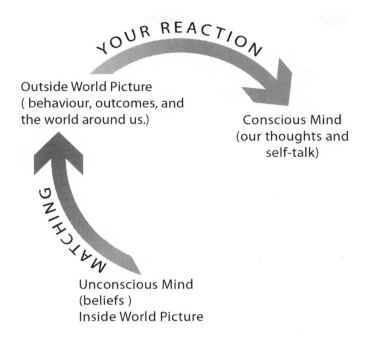

And remember, the unconscious mind doesn't know the difference between what's real and what's imagined. So with this barrage of insults, it's not like you've procrastinated once. To the unconscious mind, you've procrastinated dozens and dozens of times.

More repetition.

By beating yourself up with "negative self-talk," you are giving consent and mustering up a good deal of negative emotion . . .

Which, completes the cycle and reinforces this belief in your unconscious mind.

You reinforce the belief. You remind the unconscious mind who you are and how you act and so the next time the opportunity arises for you to procrastinate, you most certainly will do it . . . and the cycle continues.

Dana Wilde

And that is The Cycle of Perpetual Sameness.

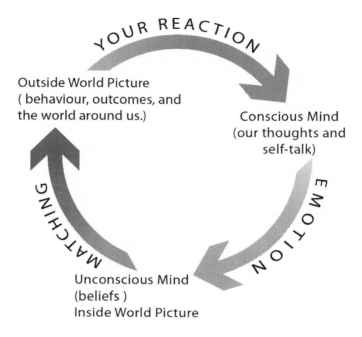

Remember when I said we often give our unconscious mind carte blanche to do as it pleases? Well, even though a belief may be limiting us, every time we address this issue through negative self-talk, we're agreeing with this belief; we're giving consent. We're reinforcing this belief.

And that's why it's so important to not let your unconscious beliefs go "unchecked." Train Your Brain teaches you to be keenly aware of "signals" that tell you when to pay more attention to your thoughts and emotions or when you are engaging in counter-productive or negative self-talk.

I call this process "removing the blinders." Noted psychologist, Carl Jung, called it "making the unconscious conscious"—which means bringing unconscious thought patterns into your conscious awareness.

Remember, you're using your brain to reinforce ideas about yourself and the world around you, thousands and thousands of times a day!

It's estimated the brain has between 60,000 and 90,000 thoughts per day. WOW! And of those 60,000 to 90,000 . . . Are you ready for the really scary statistic? 96% are the very same thoughts you had yesterday!

You gravitate toward certain thoughts and certain emotions, largely out of habit.

So much of your thinking is done automatically because you couldn't seriously tackle every thought going on in your head. Thoughts, emotions, and beliefs stored in the unconscious mind are nothing more than "simple agreements" you've made with the world around you. And much of your day-to-day thinking seems to happen automatically, mostly out of necessity.

Imagine the burden of having to contemplate every single thing you came across in your life each and every day. You'd go bonkers, right? Thankfully, the unconscious mind relieves you of this burden.

But that doesn't mean you've relinquished power over your thoughts, emotions, or beliefs. Quite the opposite is true.

And this is a major point I want to make in this book:

· ·

You DO have "absolute control" over your
thoughts, emotions, and beliefs, and they can be
changed to your benefit at any moment.
This is your choice.

No one can think in your head

· ·

Dana Wilde

Needless to say, you've leaned on your unconscious mind for good reason, but now it's time to have your conscious mind do the good work needed to "make positive change" and catapult your business forward.

Again, the real key is becoming aware of beliefs that limit your success in any way.

It might be procrastinating . . . or it might be anxiety in talking to potential customers . . . or a fear of technology . . . or a hesitation to implement strategies that could help you build your business.

Whatever your belief, in almost every case, a belief that limits your business or gets in the way of your success can be overcome, simply and effortlessly. It's getting your mind aware that you are always in control of what you feel, what you think and what you believe.

It also means stop berating yourself for having negative or counterproductive emotions and beliefs. It's like salting a wound. So give yourself a break.

Allowing yourself to make mistakes along the way creates even more room to navigate through all your different thoughts, emotions, and beliefs at your own pace.

Train Your Brain has created "shortcuts" to help you make positive change with less effort and less time so more of your time is spent increasing your business and transforming your life.

In the past we were told beliefs in the unconscious mind were permanent. Basically, we were told, we were pretty much "stuck with our beliefs," which isn't true.

Sure, we all know, if repeated in our minds or left unchecked, beliefs can appear to be permanent, but we also know beliefs are adaptable and ever-changing, if we "choose" them to be.

Current research shows the mind as extremely pliable and changeable. By flexing your mind muscles you can easily change your beliefs and create positive, desired outcomes for your business simply, quickly, and effectively.

Beliefs are powerful. Beliefs affect your life, both positively and negatively. And you want your beliefs to be positive, solid and strong. You wouldn't want them any other way. But you still want to be able to change them when you see fit. Now you can.

Bringing new information into your conscious awareness affirms that good, positive change is possible and guarantees that eliminating old, unwanted beliefs won't take a ton of effort on your part.

Remember, beliefs are created by the simple choices you make, and they are changed by those same simple choices.

CHAPTER 15

MAKING CHANGE

Before we begin discussing making change, I'd like to remind you that the unconscious mind is pliable and changeable.

Now, there are three basic ways to change your behavior, develop new habits, or change your self-images. You can make change at the unconscious level, the behavioral level and the conscious level. Making change in one of these three ways is what I like to call, "interrupting the cycle", because we are interrupting the Cycle of Perpetual Sameness.

Changing behavior at the unconscious level entails some type of hypnotherapy or self-directed hypnosis to "access" your unconscious mind and change beliefs already stored and solidified in your brain.

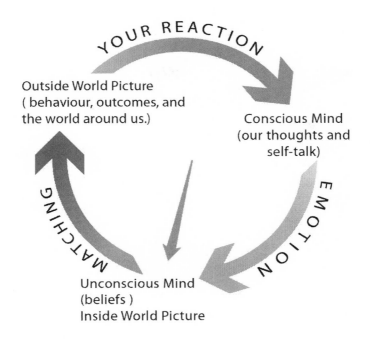

Outside World Picture
(behaviour, outcomes, and
the world around us.)

Conscious Mind
(our thoughts and
self-talk)

Unconscious Mind
(beliefs)
Inside World Picture

Hypnotherapy and self-hypnosis are both very effective and safe methods, but I will not be addressing these methods in this section.

Interrupting the cycle can also happen at the behavior level. This is sometimes called behavior modification. In short, modifying your behavior means forcing yourself to act in a different manner. When you want to change a habit, you just stop the habit for a period of time or force yourself to behave differently in order to transform your behavior, your body, or your lifestyle. This is a very popular method for change, but not very effective. Why?

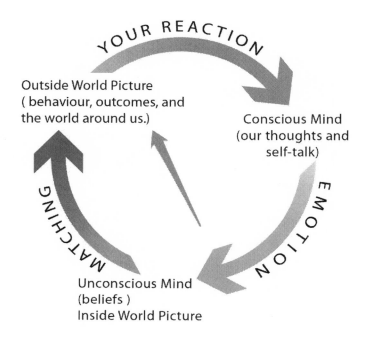

YOUR REACTION

Outside World Picture
(behaviour, outcomes, and
the world around us.)

Conscious Mind
(our thoughts and
self-talk)

EMOTION

MATCHING

Unconscious Mind
(beliefs)
Inside World Picture

The main problem with trying to change your lifestyle at the behavior level is that, over time, you usually revert to your old behavior. Changing behavior is extremely difficult, and it takes a lot of conscious effort to act out of accordance with beliefs stored in the unconscious mind. The little matchmaker in your head is continually matching the outside world to your inside world and so there is comfort in reverting back to your old ways because that behavior matches your inside world picture.

Lou Tice, when talking about making change at the behavior level says the mind acts "like a boat on automatic pilot." The boat is already "programmed" to go in a specific direction and speed.

Now, granted, it's certainly possible to grab the steering wheel and force the boat in a different direction, but when you let go of the steering wheel, the boat will quickly revert back to its original programming.

And this is how your unconscious mind works. If you force yourself to do something that is "out of sync" with your unconscious programming, it's easy for the mind and body to revert back to the old ways.

Finally, the third method for interrupting the cycle occurs at the conscious level. With this technique we simply use our conscious mind to reprogram the unconscious mind. We stop that negative self-talk and we reprogram the unconscious mind with new messages.

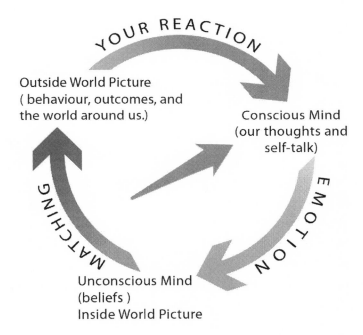

Making change at the conscious level is by far the easiest of the three. Why? Because these techniques can be implemented immediately, and their effectiveness never wears off. By the end of this book you will become an expert at using this method to make changes in your life and we'll begin immediately in this module.

CHAPTER 16

THE FIRST STEPS TO CHANGE

I think it's become obvious by now that most people are on a continuous cycle of acting on a belief, engaging in negative self-talk, which reinforces the belief, which means they act on it again.

So in order to create change in our lives, we have to interrupt the cycle somewhere and as we discussed earlier, the best place for change to occur is at the conscious level. Creating different outcomes in your life begins by paying attention to your thoughts and then changing your thoughts to productive or positive thoughts in order to reprogram the unconscious mind.

In order to make changes, you need to see why you're getting the results you're getting now and so step one in this process of interrupting the cycle is to start paying attention to what you're saying to yourself. What kind of thoughts are you having in your head right now?

Do they sound like this?

> "I'm so busy."
> "I don't have any time to do what I want to do."
> "Where does the time go?"
> "I'm so stressed out."

"I'm so overwhelmed."

"I wish I had more time."

"We always seem to be short on cash."

"I wish I could get out of debt."

"How am I ever going to pay off these credit cards?"

"I'd like to buy that, but I can't right now."

"I wish I could get out from under all of these bills."

"We're having trouble making ends meet."

"I thought this business was going to be easier than it is."

"I can't seem to gain any traction in my business."

"No one has any money to buy my products or services."

"No one ever calls me back."

"I'm working too much to make a go of this business."

"It's too much work for the payback."

I'm sure we could list an endless string of self-defeating thoughts for just about any aspect of life, but I think you're getting the idea. These may not even be "thoughts". You may actually be saying these things out loud to the people around you.

Remember, this is your inside picture of the world. At this moment in time . . . this is who you are and where you are with your business.

So step one is to get very, very aware of the thoughts you are saying to yourself and in Mindware Experiment #3, we get into this process in much more detail.

As you pay attention to your thought, try to be objective and just observe your thoughts, like a scientist would observe them.

Step Two—Decide to Change

Remember, 96% of your daily thoughts are repeated and this is why many times your future can mirror your present with only small incremental changes.

If you want to change your future you have to wrap your heads around a few things:

You cannot change your future with the same kind of thinking which created your present. This means, whatever situations you are presently experiencing, both good and not so good, are the direct result of what you were thinking last month, last week, and yesterday.

You can't create your own success by telling yourself over and over again . . . you aren't going to make it . . . you don't have what it takes to be successful . . . or it's too difficult to build a business.

You can't get rich by talking about how broke you are.

You can't find peace of mind by focusing on how overwhelmed or stressed out you are.

You will not become successful in your business by talking about all the obstacles standing in your way.

This just makes sense, doesn't it?

So Step 1 is to start paying attention to what you're saying to yourself. Step 2 is to decide to change that message. Decide to interrupt the cycle.

One tip that helps me a lot when I'm implementing these two steps . . . If I catch myself saying or thinking something counter-productive, I usually just ask myself, "Is this the message I want to match?" It's a continual reminder that the choice is mine.

You may continue reading or go to part two of this book and play with Mindware Experiment #3—Observing Thoughts.

CHAPTER 17

IMPLEMENTING MANTRAS

By now I have no doubt that you're beginning to see more clearly how the mind works and why most people only have small or incremental change in their lives and businesses. I also am sure that you've been able to look at your own life and your own outcomes and "make the match" to your inside thoughts.

And finally by now I'm sure it's crystal clear that in order to have substantial change, the type of change that affects your life dramatically, you must begin to feed your brain "different" thoughts.

You learned that step one to making change is to pay attention to your thoughts and step two is to "decide" to change or decide to interrupt the cycle.

Well, step three is to install new programming, the new belief, into the unconscious mind by using mantras and perfect language.

I'm guessing you may have already heard the term "affirmations" before. During the self-help movement of the 1970s and '80s, affirmations really came to the forefront of American culture. And, depending on your age, you might recall the Saturday Night Live character Stuart

Smalley satirizing affirmations, saying, "I'm good enough. I'm smart enough and doggone it, people like me."

(If you don't know Stuart Smalley, he's alive and well on YouTube and very funny.)

You may have heard of affirmations before or perhaps you've heard affirmations called incantations or declarations. In Train Your Brain, they are called "mantras", but all of these words are describing the same thing. Simply put, a mantra is a short positive phrase depicting a desired outcome.

Mantra is a Sanskrit word given to sacred words, chants, or sounds used during meditation to facilitate spiritual power and capable of transforming consciousness.

Whew! Sounds "out there," huh? Facilitating spiritual power? Transforming consciousness?

Well, that's exactly what you are doing when you're saying your mantras and making your positive declarations.

Even though Train Your Brain reaches far beyond mantras and affirmations, I've included them in this book because of their simplicity and effectiveness.

Mantras are useful for two reasons:

1) Mantras keep your mind occupied with positive information. Contrary to popular belief, you cannot think two thoughts at the same time. If your mind is occupied with a positive mantra, it's less time you're thinking of a negative situation.

2) Mantras reprogram your unconscious mind in the same way you were programmed in the first place—through repetition and emotion—this is also the same way you learned to pick up an object and the same way you learned a negative belief about yourself.

If I could teach only one technique for training your brain, I would pick this one . . . the implementation of an effective mantra written in perfect language.

A mantra is a foundational tool for change. When you begin to implement mantras in your business you will see results.

Part of the reason we start our process for change with learning how to create and implement a mantra is because it helps us to understand "perfect language."

Perfect language is language that makes affirmative statements more effective and accelerates change in our outside world picture.

One reason mantras and affirmations created with perfect language became so prominent and remain such a successful phenomenon today is because they were built upon a basic truth about how the brain works.

That is, the unconscious mind cannot distinguish between what's real and what's imagined. Each and every thought we have is accepted as fact.

The beauty of mantras is that you're utilizing the brain's natural tendencies to your advantage. You aren't changing how the brain works. You couldn't even if you tried. That'd be like trying to change how the heart or kidney works.

It doesn't matter whether you're putting negative or counterproductive thoughts in your brain or whether you're implanting affirmative or positive statements; the brain processes all your thoughts in the same way.

The brain processes the information, creates beliefs in the unconscious mind, an then looks to match those beliefs with the outside world.

Mantras can be spoken out loud or said silently. Either way they are effective. You might say them to your kids, to your cats, to your dogs or to yourself. Use whichever method works best for you. Any which way, mantras work.

Mantra is just a pretty name for a "positive conscious thought" and when you're saying a mantra you're really just declaring a goal for yourself, something that is truthful and within your reach.

So implementing mantras into your lifestyle is a way to make your brain more resourceful and productive so you find better opportunities for your business.

To be clear, mantras and perfect language are used in one of two ways:

1) Interrupting the Cycle. In the heat of a moment when you catch yourself using negative language or engaging in a negative self-talk, you can change your self-talk immediately and implement a perfect language mantra that is positive and better reflects the outcome you'd like to achieve.
2) Ongoing. You can create one powerful, personal, perfect language mantra to say repeatedly during your day on an ongoing basis, whenever you think of it.

You will learn more about implementing both of these methods in upcoming Mindware Experiments. Either way, mantras are powerful.

In the next chapter, we'll get into the specifics of perfect language and how to create your own mantra.

CHAPTER 18

UNDERSTANDING PERFECT LANGUAGE

In the last chapter we talked about the power of mantras and specifically perfect language mantras and so in this section we want to explain perfect language.

As you progress through the Train Your Brain book, you will discover ways to modify perfect language so that your mantras always feel natural to you, but as a starting point, you must understand the Train Your Brain concept of "perfect language."

Perfect language capitalizes on what we already know about how the brain works and uses that knowledge to our advantage. There are four basic guidelines for perfect language mantras:

1) Make your statement in the positive.
2) Make your statement as though it has already happened or already been resolved.
3) Make your statement believable.
4) Go for the positive emotional impact. Avoid wishy-washy language.

Let's look at each guideline in more detail.

Number one, make your statement in the positive.

Have you heard the saying, "Don't think about pink elephants"? As you probably just experienced, the second you hear that sentence, the very FIRST thing you think of is pink elephants! In fact, it's nearly impossible to NOT think of pink elephants.

This is a clear example of how the brain works. The brain thinks in pictures and it's always focusing on the "main subject" of your statements. It focuses on the main subject, whether you're talking about something in the positive or in the negative.

So therefore, when you hear, "Don't think about pink elephants," you immediately see the picture in your mind of the main subject of that sentence . . . pink elephants.

Here are some other good examples of this phenomena and as you read each of these sentences, see if you can identify the pictures appearing in your mind:

If you hear to the statement, "I want to be out of debt," the first thing that comes to mind is, debt.

On the other hand, if you hear the statement, "I'm financially abundant," you immediately picture yourself financially abundant.

Looking more closely at the main subject of your mantra will help you create a more positive and, thus, more effective statement.

Rather than saying or thinking, "I don't want to work so much." You can say or think, "I have plenty of free time."

Instead of, "I don't want negative customers," state "My clients are positive and supportive."

Go ahead and play with this for yourself. It's easy if you remember to focus on what you want and not what you "don't" want. Focus on your main subject and always make the main subject something positive or constructive.

Let's move on to guideline number two.

Guideline number two for perfect language is to make your statement as though it has already happened or has already been resolved.

State the situation as if the problem was resolved or fixed. If the problem were resolved, who would you be? What would you be doing? What would you have?

So state your mantras as though these circumstances exist for you right now.

For example, if you say, "I'm going to have a financially profitable business" or "I want to have a financially profitable business," it sounds like that situation will happen sometime in the future. When exactly?

Soon? Some day? Next year? Ten years from now?

Remember that the filter in your unconscious mind, the Reticular Activating System, wants to match the outside world picture to your inside world picture. If your inside picture says that you are "going to" or that you "want to" have a financially profitable business in the future, then that is exactly what your unconscious mind will match . . . something profitable in the future . . . but not now.

So it's very important to always state your mantras as though they've already happened. State them as though they exist for you now.

If you were to make the statement, "I have a financially profitable business," now your unconscious mind gets busy matching THAT picture!

This might seem like a bit of a leap for you right now but, as you practice perfect language, it will get easier and easier. Soon you will get the hang of using perfect language and when you do, nothing packs a punch like stating your mantra as though it has already happened.

The point is, you want your "new statement" to be powerful and bold enough to elicit some strong emotion inside you or have enough emotional weight to make it into your unconscious mind. Basically, you want to give your unconscious mind something to "work with."

"I have a financially profitable business" feels exciting and confident. "I'm going to have a financially profitable business" feels distant, iffy and leaves room for doubt.

Eliminate certain phrases like "I'm going to" and "I want to" from your vocabulary. These types of words don't give your conscious mind much to work with; they're too vague or wishy-washy or iffy.

I know when you first start playing with perfect language, it may sound unrealistic or a bit contrived to you. It may feel like a huge leap. This is a common feeling.

As I mentioned earlier, we will give you some other tools in later sections which will help you to modify perfect language so that it feels more natural to you, but in the meantime, bear with me for a moment, because learning how to use perfect language when creating your mantras will prepare you for making that huge leap down the road.

As I said in the beginning, I want to teach this material to you in the very same way I learned it; and understanding the nuances of the different ways we talk to ourselves is another simple step in the process of learning how to train your brain.

Alright, on to guideline number three . . .

Guideline number three is to make your statements believable.

In the past when people created mantras, they often made statements "out of reach" from where they were in their current situation. People making $15,000 a year might say an affirmation like, "I make a million dollars a year" over and over, but when nothing changed and they didn't increase their income, they'd say, "those stupid affirmations don't work!"

If you make a statement such as, "I make a million dollars a year," your loyal best friend the unconscious mind will immediately respond to your newest declaration by saying, "Yes, of course, you make a million dollars a year!"

On the other hand, your conscious mind is not such a good friend sometimes. Remember the rolling pin? Your conscious mind hears the statement, "I make a million dollars a year" and quickly chimes in, "Geez! Yeah, right. Sure you do, dummy. More like a million cents a year!"

So, you want to slip under the radar of the conscious mind by making your statements believable. To be clear, you won't always literally "believe" what you're saying in your mantra, but you want your statements to be believable enough that they get past the watchful eye of your conscious mind, which, functioning like a radar, will quickly hone in and berate you for saying any outlandish or unrealistic ideas.

Obviously, believability is a little tricky, and you'll learn more about this as you continue with Train Your Brain. Everyone has a different barometer for what is believable in a mantra. Trust your instinct about what is realistic for you to make your affirmations more effective.

On to guideline number four . . . go for the positive emotional impact.

No matter which subject we are discussing, Train Your Brain always seems to loop back to emotion and there is a very good reason for this. Emotion is everything.

Remember mantras are useful for two reasons:

1) Mantras keep your mind occupied with positive information.
2) Mantras reprogram your unconscious mind in the same way you were programmed in the first place—through repetition and emotion.

. . . .

The only power in your mantra comes
from the emotion it generates in you.

. . . .

The reason you say mantras is because they help you to feel good! The only power in your mantra comes from the emotion it generates in you.

When you feel good your mind is more creative and resourceful. When you feel good you identify better opportunities. When you feel good you take action and not just any kind of action, but effective action that reaps positive results. It all starts with feeling good.

Therefore, you want to create mantras using this fourth guideline. You want to go for the positive emotional impact.

One way to do this is to eliminate certain words or phrases from your mantras. Words like "try," "might" or "wish" and phrases that I mentioned earlier like "I'm going to" or "I want to."

You want to use strong, definitive language. You always want to ask yourself, "How does this statement make me feel?" Does it make me feel excited? Ready to go?

Take a look at the following statements. Next say them out loud and see if you can feel the emotional difference between each statement.

> "I wish I had a million dollar business."
> "I want to have a million dollar business."
> "I'm going to have a million dollar business."

Did you notice the subtle and not-so-subtle difference in the emotional impact of each statement?

In the first statement, "I wish I had a million dollar business," can you see how this might make you feel that having a million dollar business is just a pipedream?

Look closely at the second statement: "I want to have a million dollar business." Although saying this could make you feel a bit better because the word want suggests a stronger possibility of having a million dollar business, you're still not feeling entirely sure this will happen.

And if you say, "I'm going to have a million dollar business" you might feel like you're on your way but, still, saying this most likely won't evoke feelings of complete certainty.

So if you want to create a strong, effective affirmation using perfect language, you would bypass all three options and simply say, "I have a million dollar business."

This "new statement" fulfills all the guidelines for a good mantra. It's a statement in the positive. It's stated as though it's already happened. It may be believable for the right person. It has emotional impact and avoids all those wishy-washy words like "try, might, wish, and want."

Here's the bottom line: What would it feel like if you actually had a million dollar business right now? If having a million dollar business were your goal, what feelings would you experience when you achieved this goal? Excited? Happy? Confident?

It's those types of positive emotions that you want to generate with your mantras.

Again, these four guidelines help explain how to use perfect language with your mantras. Nobody thinks or talks perfectly. But this section on perfect language is important, because it shows how the subtle differences in your positive statements will improve your mantras; and, more importantly, it helps you become more aware of what feelings are stimulated by the words you use.

All four of these guidelines explain how to effectively use perfect language to your advantage. You will have an opportunity to create your own perfect language mantra in Mindware Experiment #5 and so stay tuned.

Implementing perfect language mantras will help you create new thinking and new ways of talking to yourself and they will imprint your unconscious mind with new beliefs.

You may continue reading or go to part two of this book and play with Mindware Experiment #4—Turn It Around, as well as Mindware Experiment #5—Create Your Own Mantra.

CHAPTER 19

HEIDI'S STORY

Several years ago I was speaking at a sales conference and a woman named Heidi approached me in the hotel lobby and told me an amazing story. I think her story really illustrates the power of creating "super-charged" mantras using perfect language.

Heidi was an independent consultant for a direct sales company and she informed me that a fellow consultant suggested using one of my methods to move her business forward.

"And so I did," she said, bursting with energy.

I said, "Great, which one?"

Heidi started telling me her story. She started by saying that some months ago, she had become increasingly depressed about her direct selling business, often telling other consultants in the company that she couldn't ever see herself becoming an Executive Director, a level of achievement in her company.

She told me she'd been with her company for many years and didn't really feel she was sponsoring enough people. Even when she did sponsor someone, the person wouldn't place any orders or would go inactive. She said she couldn't imagine meeting the requirements of sponsoring 15 people who would order enough to stay active.

But she said another consultant, who had attended a Train Your Brain live training, suggested she just start saying to herself over and over again . . . "I'm an Executive Director."

Heidi leaned in toward me awkwardly, as if guarding herself from embarrassment. She said, "Dana, you can't imagine how ridiculous this sounded to me at first. But I figured I had nothing to lose. So I started saying it all the time, dozens, even hundreds of times a day!"

I laughed. Then Heidi said she and her husband started saying it to each other out loud and they'd actually say it out loud as a way of kidding around with each other. She said, "Even though I didn't take it seriously at first, it sure was making me feel better. And I knew there was a part of me that believed it."

I immediately asked, "Believed what?"

"That I'm an Executive Director," Heidi said.

"Awesome!" I said.

But Heidi wasn't done telling her story.

Nine months had passed since she first started repeating "I'm an Executive Director," and she revealed that today she received a phone call from someone she's been talking to about her business. "She wants to sign up tomorrow," Heidi said.

"And guess what? When she signs up with me tomorrow, she will be the fifteenth first—level team member I've sponsored, and I will finally become an Executive Director FOR REAL!"

To say Heidi had a look of utter joy on her face would be an understatement!

I stayed in touch with Heidi and she went on to use mantras to earn a company car bonus and other prestigious company awards.

Heidi's story is just one of countless testimonials we receive from people using Train Your Brain techniques. However, an interesting note about Heidi's story is that even though she wasn't sure she believed what she was saying would work, just the act of saying the words "I'm an Executive Director" made her feel good.

This is a really important point. Even though she didn't fully believe her mantra when she started, she knew it was "attainable" for her and this made it believable enough. Over time, she believed it more and more.

Her story is also a testimony to the importance of saying a mantra that feels good. If saying a mantra makes you feel better, you're on the right track. As Heidi has proven, mantras can come true if created with genuine good feeling.

Heidi's story really is amazing. She had been trying for years without much success and achieved a monumental goal in nine months by creating one "perfect" statement—that's truly remarkable!

In fact, Heidi's amazing story makes the Mindware Experiments seem like we're dealing with magic. Because when success hits us like it did for Heidi, it can feel magical

But it's not magic.

Your mind is so powerful that when you reprogram or rewrite what you think, how you feel, what you believe, you're essentially creating an entirely "new" outside picture of the world for yourself. And if watching your life transform before your own eyes isn't truly magical, it sure comes close.

CHAPTER 20

DANA'S MANTRA STORY

Since we've been talking about mantras and direct sales stories, I thought I would tell you my story about my direct sales teams' rise to the Million Dollar Club in nineteen months. It clearly shows how powerful mantras and using perfect language can literally transform your business and your life.

Many years ago, like many people in direct sales and network marketing, I attended an in-home party and became excited about the products presented that evening. In fact, I became so excited I signed up to be a Consultant.

In the beginning stages of my business, I did parties by closely following the instructions in our company's training manual. The training manual said, "Present the business opportunity at the beginning, middle, and end of the party," so I did. At the end of my third month of doing parties, I signed my first team member.

Needless to say, I was thrilled.

Signing people into the business seemed to come pretty easily for me, and I signed several more over the next month or so. Right around that time, one of the senior members in the company called me. She told me that I had an opportunity to break the company record for the fastest rise to Executive Director.

To be an Executive Director, a person had to personally sponsor fifteen Consultants into the business and the quickest anyone had ever done this at the time was six months. I thought, "Cool! I'm going to do that!"

As I continued doing my parties, I was pretty excited about how well things were going and how fast I was sponsoring new Consultants. I wanted to tell people how excited I was that I was on target to have the fastest rise to Executive Director in the history of the company, but I couldn't do it because it felt like bragging to say, "Hey, you know what? I made Executive Director faster than anyone."

I was proud of the success I was attaining, but my mother raised me to be humble and I just couldn't bring myself to talk about this impending achievement so openly.

So instead, as I was presenting the opportunity at my parties, I just started saying, "This is the fastest growing team in the history of the company." I'd usually follow it up with something like, "Now is the time to join, because this is the fastest growing team in the history of the company."

This spontaneous phrase became a very effective mantra for me. I didn't have to feel sheepish about bragging and, more importantly, I felt great when I said it!

And of course as I would add new team members, they would in turn start saying this same mantra at their parties. They heard me say it and so they repeated it too. This little mantra of mine caught on with every new person coming onto my new team. It became a "team mantra." In fact, this mantra became so contagious it went viral!

If our team members said, "We're the fastest growing team in the history of the company" once, we probably said it ten thousand times!

To be honest, I really had no "evidence" that we were the fastest growing team in the history of the company. Our company didn't recognize team sales, so there was no concrete way to gauge if we truly were the fastest growing team. I guess it really didn't matter if it was a fact. I believed we were the fastest growing team! Call me crazy, but I knew it with every fiber of my being! And it felt great!

And so a short nineteen months after I purchased my distributor kit, our team was recognized, in fact, as the fastest team to reach the million dollars in yearly sales mark in the history of our company. We didn't just break the company record, we shattered it, and the record still stands today.

I often tell people we broke the record by accident. What I mean is, when I started out I did not sit down with a pen and paper and write down goals. I did not develop a plan. I did not make a vision board. I didn't even write a list of mantras. I just latched on to one little mantra that felt good when I said it.

In fact, it's worth noting that I did a whole list of things completely wrong when I started my direct sales business. For example, I did not have business cards until I was with the company for six months. I was already at the executive level in the company before I created a business card. I did not know how to present or explain our most popular product until I was with the company for almost nine months. I did not do a team newsletter until I was with the company for two years! I didn't recognize team members' sales. I did not play party games, a staple in the party plan industry, and I taught my team members to do the same for the first two years of my business. I could go on and on. I made mistake after mistake when starting up my business, but I did one thing very right . . . I had a strong mantra and unending focus for saying it.

I'll share more about our team's story when I delve deeper into emotions later. But I wanted to share this part because it emphasizes how easily success can flow to you when you make a decision to bring something new into your conscious awareness—like a new mantra. And, when you feel good about your new line of thinking, you end up believing in what you say so strongly that this powerful feeling becomes second nature to you and you never question again whether you will be successful.

When this happens for you, I guarantee, you will never feel like you need to go back to that old way of thinking ever again.

You may continue reading or go to part two of this book and play with Mindware Experiment #6—Bombard Yourself With Post-It Notes

CHAPTER 21

FREQUENTLY ASKED QUESTIONS ABOUT MANTRAS

As people start to work with mantras, similar questions arise and so I wanted to address a few of these questions in this chapter.

Question: I've heard when you're visualizing you should try to be specific. Should I be specific in my mantra?

Answer: If it's possible for you to be specific in your mantra and feel really good when you say it, then be specific, but that's not usually the case for most people.

Many times, when you think of an idea for a mantra, you get excited and you feel good. Often, if you take it a step further and start thinking of all of the details and specifics surrounding the situation addressed in your mantra, your conscious mind starts to get the rolling pin out and starts telling you all the reasons why your idea will never work.

For this reason, contrary to popular opinion, being more general in your mantras works better. Always remember, the single most important thing about a mantra is that it feels good.

For example, if my mantra had been, "we grew to the million dollar level in 19 months," as each month passed, I would have been more and more freaked out about attaining that goal . . . negative feelings that are very counter productive to success!

So, for most people, it's best to use a more general mantra like these examples . . .

> "Business is booming!"
> "Money is flowing to me now!"
> "My business is growing by leaps and bounds!"
> "Calling my customers is easy!"

Now, if you are able to be more specific and still maintain those high-flying feelings, then by all means, get specific! Many times as people get closer and closer to attaining a goal, their mantra will get more and more specific.

Again, if you remember that feeling good is paramount, you will have success with your mantra.

Question: How many times a day should I say my mantra?

Answer: You should say your mantra as many times as you think of it throughout the day.

One habit that is great to develop is to say your mantra (out loud or silently to yourself) 25 times first thing in the morning. This is a terrific way to make sure you are saying it every day. However, if for any reason you don't develop this as a habit, ease your mind, mantras will still work for you.

Whenever possible, implement Mindware Experiment #6 and add post it notes with your written mantra to your surroundings. This will help you to remember to say it.

Another great trick is to set an alarm on your mobile phone that notifies you to say it at regular intervals.

Throughout your day when you catch yourself thinking ordinary, mundane thoughts, say to yourself, "This would be the perfect time to say my mantra!" When you're doing the dishes, brushing your teeth, sitting at stop lights in the car, taking out the garbage, or during any other routine task where you usually allow your mind to go on automatic pilot, catch yourself and say your mantra.

One thing is for sure . . . you cannot say it too often

Question: How long do I have to say my mantra?

Answer: Say your mantra until you attain the goal you were planning to reach or change it or tweak it any time you think changing it would give you greater emotional impact.

Sometimes if you've been saying a mantra for a while, you'll notice that you're just "going through the motions" and you don't have any real emotional attachment to the mantra. If you catch yourself in a situation like this, make sure to change up your mantra. I can't say it enough, emotion is everything.

Question: How many mantras can I have?

Answer: When you are first working with mantras, you may be trying several mantras that are similar at the same time. For example:

> "My business is growing by leaps and bounds!"
> "Growing my business is so easy!"
> "My business is growing so fast!"
> "I love my fast growing business!"

You may want to practice with several mantras of the same style to see which one feels best. Very quickly, you'll discover that one will stand out and this will become your main mantra and your main focus.

With regards to having several mantras covering different areas of life, see the next question.

Question: Can I have multiple mantras for different areas of my life?

Answer: Many times when someone learns about mantras, they want to start using them to improve every area of their life!

Here are the facts regarding variety in your mantras . . .

Brain scientists say the brain can handle up to three different topics. So, for example, you could have a mantra about your business, a mantra about your relationship, and a mantra about your health.

However, in my personal experience in working with thousands of small business owners, I would highly recommend that when you first start out, you start with just one mantra (or at the most two mantras.)

The reason I recommend this is because it will cause you to focus and when you focus, you will see the changes to your outside world happen more quickly. When changes happen quickly it gives you confidence to try other mantras.

In later sections we will give you some additional tricks for covering multiple topics with one mantra, but I highly recommend when you start out to just stick with one well-crafted mantra that makes you feel really, really good!

CHAPTER 22

TRANSITORY STATEMENTS

When I first started presenting Train Your Brain for live audiences, often someone in the audience would say to me, "I've tried affirmations in the past and I feel like I'm lying to myself."

Feeling as though you're "lying" to yourself when you're saying your mantra is a common issue and I promise I'll address this issue in a moment.

But first, let me start with section by saying that most of us are already lying to ourselves hundreds, if not thousands, of times a day.

What I mean by that is that we are already, most certainly, projecting less-than-positive, less-than-true thoughts about ourselves more often than we'd like to admit.

Think about it, how many times have you told yourself you weren't good enough, or smart enough for something? And how many times have you thought you just didn't have what it takes to be successful in the business world?

If this is not lying, I don't know what is. The vast majority of us do this in some form or another on a daily basis. The point is, when we think negative thoughts like these, we are not only lying to ourselves, but we're also experiencing thoughts that don't feel very good.

However, having said all of that, because "believability" is such an important part of reprogramming the unconscious mind, I want to introduce my concept of Transitory Statements.

Earlier, I talked about the mantra, "I make a million dollars a year!" Do you remember how I said the unconscious mind agrees wholeheartedly with this statement? That's how our indiscriminate and loyal friend, the unconscious mind, reacts. But remember, I also said the conscious mind will always "call our bluff" and if the statement is not "believable", the conscious mind will immediately disagree and start berating us.

Well, if you're having this challenge when you use a perfect language mantra, you might have better luck using a Transitory Statement.

It probably goes without saying that I don't want you to give up on your mantra or any other type of positive statement you might create, but sometimes you may be dealing with an area of your life where you don't feel sure of yourself. Sometimes you feel confident enough to make audacious statements. Other times, making bold statements such as, "I have a financially profitable business!" or "Business is booming!" might feel close to lying.

Therefore, as a general rule, remember . . .

Any thought you're thinking is only as "valuable" as the feeling it generates inside you.

In other words, emotion is your indicator. How you feel when you say your mantra will determine if using perfect language is appropriate for you. If it feels good, perfect language is well . . . perfect. If it feels like you're lying to yourself, then use a Transitory Statement.

Transitory Statements do not necessarily use perfect language, but they are effective because they feel good when you say them. They point you in the right direction. You can think of Transitory Statements as "stepping stones" on your way to perfect language.

Transitory Statements are created in one of three ways:

1) Keep the image, but change the message.
2) Link the change to an event.
3) State the change as though it is in progress.

I'll explain each of these three styles in the upcoming chapters and show you how you can implement Transitory Statements to create change in your life.

CHAPTER 23

KEEP THE IMAGE, CHANGE THE MESSAGE

The first type of Transitory Statement I'd like to address is what I like to call "keep the image, but change the message."

If you've been picturing yourself in a certain way for a long time, sometimes it's difficult to just flip a switch and see yourself in a different light. If you've spent your whole life seeing yourself as a disorganized person or a shy person or a headstrong person, you identify yourself so deeply with that character trait, it's so much a part of "who you are", that it often seems impossible to change.

In addition, sometimes as a culture, we label some character traits as "better" than others. We think that it's necessary to "be a certain way" in order to be successful. Entire books have been written on this subject alone!

And so what sometimes happens is that if you don't possess those certain special character traits that everyone attributes to success, it's easy to feel like either you will never achieve success or you have to change your personality in order to be successful. Neither choice sounds very pleasant.

Well, the first type of Transitory Statement helps you to "keep the image, but change the message."

For instance, let's use shyness as an example. Let's say you are someone who is shy and as an entrepreneur, you know that a good part of your future success is contingent on spreading the word about your business. Marketing your business might include one-on-one meetings or group presentations or networking in large crowds.

In addition, you may have been raised in a culture in which introverts or shy people are not expected to do well in marketing or networking, and so you may be having an internal dialog, which sounds like this:

> "I'm too shy to be successful in business."
> "All the really good marketers are extroverted."
> "Because I'm shy, I may never make a lot of money in my
>   business, but I still believe in my mission."
> "I'm good at other aspects of the business, but I'm too shy to
>   be a good marketer."

With this type of self-talk or internal dialog, you would be reinforcing the image of yourself as shy, which in and of itself is not a negative character trait. However, you would also be inadvertently reinforcing the image that an introverted person cannot succeed because of their shy nature.

If you're a shy person and you have been extremely shy and introverted your entire life, to expect you to begin saying a mantra now such as, "I am an extrovert," would be absurd. It would be nearly impossible for a perfect language mantra like this to feel believable.

So in developing a Transitory Statement, you are able to keep a comfortable or familiar image about yourself, but change the message of your statement. This allows you to create a statement with believability.

As a shy person, your Transitory Statement might sound like this:

> "I'm shy, but the presentation fits well with my style and
> customers love these products."
> "I'm really shy, but I'm successful because I attract customers
> that like my style."
> "I'm really shy, but growing my business is easy. My products
> sell themselves!"
> "I'm shy, but it's okay, because most of the time, customers
> are approaching me!"
> "I'm shy, but my personality attracts high paying customers."

These Transitory Statements don't give up on the idea of being shy, nor are they forcing you to start thinking of yourself as an extrovert. If you're a shy person, the Transitory Statements above allow your "true character" to be maintained and yet they feel good. You don't feel like you're "lying" to yourself and yet you're still creating change in your outside world picture.

Notice how each Transitory Statement above uses the word "but" in the middle of the statement. The word "but" is a very powerful word in the English language. It basically negates anything said before it. So the part of the statement getting firmly implanted in the mind is always the second half, after the word "but."

So creating a Transitory Statement is easy. You just state the situation as it is, add the word "but", and then follow the word "but" with a perfect language mantra.

Keep the image, BUT change the message.

"I'm shy, BUT I attract customers that like my style."

"I'm shy, BUT growing my business is easy!"

"I'm shy, BUT customers are approaching me!"

"I'm shy, BUT my personality attracts high paying customers."

See how that works?

Another variation of this style of Transitory Statement incorporates the words "even though" rather than "but". This time you put the words "even though" at the beginning of the sentence, so your sentences would look like this:

"Even though I'm really shy, I'm successful because I attract customers that like my style."

"Even though I'm really shy, growing my business is easy. My products sell themselves!"

"Even though I'm shy, it's okay, because most of the time, customers are approaching me!"

"Even though I'm shy, my personality attracts high paying customers."

Try both on for size. Keeping the image but changing the message is a simple yet highly effective Transitory Statement.

CHAPTER 24

LINK THE CHANGE TO AN EVENT OR ACTION

The second style of Transitory Statement is when you "link the change to an event or action."

Have you ever heard someone say something like, "I was gaining weight, but then one day I was disheartened because I was playing with my grandchild and got incredibly winded, so I lost the weight"? This is an example of someone who made lasting change in life because of a certain event (playing with a grandchild.)

Or have you ever heard someone say something like, "I used to be late for appointments, but then I started using a day planner and now I'm punctual"? This is an example of someone who made lasting change in life because of a certain action (using a day planner.)

You may have already noticed that these two sentences have a something in common . . . the words "but then" in the middle. There is our good friend, the word "but" again!

As you can see, the structure of this type of Transitory Statement is really simple.

First you state your problem as though it's in the past. For example, "I WAS gaining weight" or "I USED to be late for appointments."

Next, you insert the words "but then" or "but now" depending on the situation.

Next, you give the reason for change. Meaning you mention the event or the action which took place in order for change to occur. For example, "I was playing with my grandchild and got winded" or "I started using a day planner."

Finally, you state the new improved situation in your life. For example, "I lost the weight" or "now I'm punctual."

Remember, when you're creating Transitory Statements—or any other positive statements—think of your unconscious mind as a "mega processor," always in a state of change, ready for the next thought and the next thought and the next thought after that. You mind is ready for change at any moment and the really incredible news about the brain is that it will accept ANY reason for change.

I have often joked with clients creating this style of Transitory Statement that you can say something as ridiculous as "but then I started eating bananas on Tuesdays and blank, blank, blank change occurred" and the Transitory Statement will still work! You will see the change in your outside world. I'm really not kidding you when I say your brain will accept ANY reason for change.

Also, just like with the previous style of Transitory Statement, there is a variation you can use with this one as well. Instead of inserting "but then" in the middle of the statement, you can insert "ever since" at the beginning. This type of sentence structure would sound like this:

> "Ever since I became disheartened about being winded when
> playing with my grandchild, I lost weight."
> "Ever since I started using a day planner, I'm punctual."

Both method work and they are both effective ways to create statement that are believable.

Implement this style of Transitory Statement when you know you are attending an event or making a change in your business of any kind. It can be the smallest, most seemingly insignificant change or event, but that doesn't matter. Remember, the brain will accept ANY excuse to change.

For example, a Transitory Statement you can start saying right now would be, "Ever since I started studying Train Your Brain, I now (fill in the blank with your ideal situation.)"

And if that doesn't sound easy enough, wait until you hear this . . . remember when I said that brain will accept ANY reason for changing? Well, the brain will even accept the fact that you don't know why the change is occurring! You can literally make a Transitory Statement that sounds like this . . .

> "I don't know what I'm doing differently, but now for some
> reason, I'm _____."

I'm not kidding! Here would be some examples with the blank filled in:

> "I don't know what I'm doing differently, BUT NOW for some
> reason, I'm selling over $4,000 in product every month."
> "I don't know what has changed, BUT NOW for some
> reason, my business is growing by leaps and bounds."

"I don't know what I'm doing differently, BUT NOW for
some reason, I'm attracting a higher level of customer."

As you can see, the possibilities are endless when using this easy to
implement style of Transitory Statement. Link the change to an event
or action.

CHAPTER 25

STATE THE CHANGE AS THOUGH IT'S IN PROGRESS

The third style of Transitory Statement is when you "state the change as though it's in progress."

This one can be a little tricky to explain, but now you're getting so good at understanding how your brain works, it will be easy for you to understand.

You might remember in the section on perfect language, I talked about "making your statement as though it had already happened or had already been resolved." I talked about the importance of always remembering that the outside world picture will always match the inside world picture and so when creating perfect language mantras, you always want to give the brain something concrete to match.

What's important to remember about Transitory Statements is that we use them in areas where we don't feel comfortable using a perfect language mantra. We don't feel like the mantra is believable.

Remember Transitory Statements do not necessarily use perfect language, but they are effective because they FEEL GOOD. Remember they point you in the right direction. They are "stepping stones" on your way to perfect language.

This point will become abundantly clear when working with this third style of Transitory Statement.

Stating the change as though it's in progress means beginning your Transitory Statement with one of the following introductory phrases, and then filling in the blank with the change you'd like to see.

> "I'm getting good at _____."
> "I'm getting much better at _____."
> "I'm getting better every day at _____."
> "I'm getting better all the time at _____"
> "I'm getting pretty good _____."

With all three types of Transitory Statements you are trying to "coax" yourself into feeling better about a situation. By now you realize that real change, lasting change, starts with feeling good. Coaxing yourself into these better feelings is a great way to start creating lasting change in your business and your life.

When you say a Transitory Statement using the introductory phrases given, if it feels good and it feels believable, then it will be a success.

However, if for any reason it doesn't feel good or feel believable, you can soften the statement even one level further. You can add an introductory phrase to your introductory phrase! Here are some good examples:

> "I'm starting to notice I'm getting much better
> at _____."
> "It seems like I'm getting better all the time
> at _____"

"<u>I feel like</u> I'm getting pretty good _____."
"<u>I can see</u> I'm getting better every day at _____."
"<u>I'm seeing more and more evidence that</u> I'm getting good at _____."

Finally, if it helps to lean on our old friend, the word "but," you can do this too. Just like before, state the situation as though it's in the past, add the words "but now", and then add this third style of Transitory Statement.

If you choose to go this route, your statement might look like this:

"I used to be bad at managing my time, but now I'm getting much better at it."
"I never used to have high paying customers, but now I'm starting to notice I'm getting more clients with money."
"I used to have so many cancellations, but now it feels like things are improving."

Do you remember when I said training your brain isn't about "changing" your behavior? This is a really important point to remember when talking about this type of Transitory Statement. Always remember that you are making statements that reprogram the beliefs in your unconscious mind and they work because they feel good. You are simply coaxing yourself into a new image.

With any of our Transitory Statement styles, you only have to "say" or "think" the statement repeatedly and then feel the good feelings it generates, for it to be effective. Good feelings will take you farther in your quest to build an incredible business than anything else! You are exiting The Cycle of Perpetual Sameness.

Training your brain isn't so much about making statements with perfect language every single time. It's more about finding those statements that fit you, make you feel good and, at the same time, deliver "new information" to your brain. And if a perfect language mantra doesn't feel good or doesn't feel believable, then a Transitory Statement is an effective way to deliver the positive message to your unconscious mind.

In fact, here is a terrific Transitory Statement you can start with right now . . .

"I'm getting so good at saying positive things to myself!"

You may continue reading or go to part two of this book and play with Mindware Experiment #7—Create Your Own Transitory Statement

CHAPTER 26

THE POWER OF QUESTIONS

Have you ever struggled to find the answer to a question and, even though the answer was seemingly at the tip of your tongue, you still couldn't come up with it right away?

Usually, at that point, someone will say, "Just forget about it and it will come to you later." And that's usually what happens, isn't it?

When you stopped consciously thinking about the answer for a moment, you remember the person's name or the place or event. Oh, yeah! Now I remember!

That's a perfect example of the brain working on your behalf.

Let me give you another example . . . let's say you were attending a multi-day conference in a hotel. Every day you drove to the hotel and parked in the hotel parking lot. On day one, the speaker asks you a question from the stage. The speaker asks, "What color was the car two spots to your right in the parking lot?" You have no idea. It seems like an odd question, but when the speaker asks the audience members to raise their hand if they can answer the question, you see that barely anyone in the room raises their hand.

Day two of the conference you enter the hotel and mingle with the members of the audience before sitting down. Almost immediately, the speaker asks from the stage, "What color was the car two spots to your right in the parking lot?" You can't believe the same question is being asked and you realize again you don't know the answer. During the show of hands you see you're not alone and in fact, most of people in the room don't know the answer to the question.

On day three of the conference, you pull into the parking lot of the hotel and immediately your brain perks up and you hear a voice inside your head say, "You know the speaker is going to ask you the color of the car two spots to your right and so pay attention and take note of the color this time!" Your brain has filed away this little tidbit of information and just like a reminder bell on your mobile phone, your lovely brain alerted you to gather the information you needed.

This time when the speaker asks the question from stage and asks for a show of hands, almost every hand in the room raises. Why? It's because our handy dandy friend, our brain, is always working on our behalf to find the answers to our questions.

So whether your searching for your car keys, the name of a movie you saw, or the color of a car, your wonderful unconscious mind, always at work trying to answer your questions, goes into a "problem-solving mode," and sifts through millions of bits of information for you.

Sometimes this takes a few moments and sometimes longer, but the unconscious mind always seems to retrieve what you're trying to remember, doesn't it?

This is because questions are very powerful for the unconscious mind. And so knowing this, it's really important to pay attention to the types of questions you ask yourself and to make a conscious effort to ask yourself better questions.

Let me give you an example of how a negative question reaps negative results. Have you ever asked yourself the question, "What's my problem?" Let's think about that for a moment, "Is there really any GOOD answer to that question?" It probably goes without saying, the answer is, "No."

It's impossible to come up with a good answer to a question like that for a couple of reasons. First, asking self-defeating questions defeats the whole purpose of trying to use perfect language to create more successful positive statements and therefore more successful positive outcomes.

And second and more importantly, your unconscious mind immediately goes into problem-solving mode to answer this type of question for you. Unfortunately, this does not work to your advantage.

Ask a question like, "What's my problem?" and your loyal friend, the unconscious mind immediately starts generating a whole list of responses . . . highlighting all of your problems!

The brain is always looking for answers on your behalf and so we have created several Mindware Experiments that use the brain's natural tendency to answer questions to your advantage.

As a general rule, remember all you've learned about mantras, perfect language, and Transitory Statements up until this point and apply those same principles to any questions you ask yourself.

For example, if you hear that voice in your head say, "What's my problem?" catch yourself in the moment and see if you can turn it around using perfect language. Instead ask yourself, "What are my positive character traits?" Pay attention as you hear the flood of positive responses to that question. Other great substitutions would be:

> "What am I thankful for?"
> "What do I have going for me?"
> "What's going right in my life?"
> "What do I appreciate right now?"
> "What do I like about myself?"
> "What do others like about me?"
> "What am I happy for right now?"

Imagine all of the wonderful answers that arise when you ask powerful questions like these. So start paying attention to the questions you ask yourself and be willing to apply the principles you've learned so far to asking better questions. If you do so, your brain will jump to your aid with much better answers.

You may continue reading or go to part two of this book and play with Mindware Experiment #8—Ask A Better Question, as well as Mindware Experiment #9—Eliminating Automatic Negative Messages.

CHAPTER 27

THE WORD "BECAUSE"

By now you're getting pretty good at implanting new "mindware" into your unconscious mind. And you're learning to create the perfect language that keeps moving your business and life forward!

Now you can add one more powerful ingredient to your new messages . . . Because Statements.

The word "because" is a very powerful word in the English language. Behavioral scientist Ellen Langer actually tested the word "because" in a study conducted in a typical office, to illustrate the persuasive power of the word.

In one part of the study, Langer arranged for a stranger to approach someone waiting in line to use a photocopier and simply ask, "Excuse me, I have five pages. May I use the Xerox machine?"

Faced with a direct request to allow someone to cut in line ahead of them, 60 percent of the people were willing to allow the stranger to go ahead of themselves. However, when the same stranger made the request with a reason, asking, "May I use the Xerox machine, because I'm in a rush?" . . . almost 94 percent complied. The "sense of urgency" behind the request with the word "because" caused people to comply with a stranger's request.

Langer's team conducted a final test to cement their findings. This time, however, the stranger used the word "because" again, but then followed up because with a completely meaningless reason: "May I use the Xerox machine, because I have to make some copies?" The rate of compliance was 93 percent.

Langer's study determined that the "sense of urgency" behind a particular request had absolutely no bearing on compliance. In fact, Langer's team showed the unique power of the word "because" alone caused people to comply with a person's request, and nothing else.

This is the power of the word "because". Hearing or thinking the word "because" gives your mind a reason to accept the information as true and necessary.

So, if you want to make your mantras more powerful, you can add a "Because Statement" to the end of your mantra. When you add a Because Statement after your initial positive message, the unconscious mind automatically starts justifying why your initial positive message is "true" and accepts its validity without question.

After your initial positive message or mantra, adding your Because Statement might look like this:

Initial Positive Message or Mantra	Because Statement
"I'm financially abundant . . ."	". . . because I'm getting good at thinking positively."
"Money flows easily to me . . ."	". . . because I've learned to relax my thoughts."

Initial Positive Message or Mantra	Because Statement
"I have a million dollar business . . ."	". . . because I have amazing customer service."
"I have a full appointment calendar . . ."	". . . because I attract positive clients."
"My business is growing by leaps and bounds . . ."	". . . because I talk to everyone about my business!"

You may have noticed in these examples, your Because Statement is also a productive, positive "outcome"—something either you hope to achieve or have already achieved.

In fact, by using a Because Statement, it's almost like you are getting two mantras in one! The interesting thing we've found in working with clients at The Mind Aware is that the Because Statement can even be completely unrelated to the initial mantra. For example, you could have a Because Statement added to your mantra that sounds like this:

"I am financially abundant, because I eat healthy food every day!"

Incredibly enough, your unconscious mind gets busy and starts matching your outside world picture to BOTH of these positive messages. This is the power of the word "because."

One final word of caution . . . always be mindful of potential outcomes when wording your mantra or Because Statement. When you are programming your unconscious mind to create different outcomes in your business or your life, those outcomes will happen. So be very sure you want exactly what you ask for. The following story really illustrates this point:

I was working with a woman who had a small business. She contacted me shortly after New Year's Day and asked me to help her create a mantra.

She said, "I love my business and things are going really well, but I'm working so much. I'm working way too many hours and I think I figured out why."

Naturally, I asked, "Why?"

She told me she used a Because Statement for her mantra from the previous year, as I had suggested the previous year. Her initial mantra was, "I have grown my business to a point where I can afford to quit corporate America, because I have worked hard and asked for help."

Over the last year, because she was applying this particular mantra to her small home business and she actually had been able to quit her corporate job. However, her Because Statement was so effective that she was ALSO working hard . . . too hard!

As we discussed it, she quickly realized she was programming her unconscious mind to equate her own success with working hard. She was telling herself that things would go well only if she worked hard and unfortunately, that's exactly what came true.

Needless to say, she tweaked her Because Statement and eventually began working less and her successes didn't miss a beat!

This story absolutely reveals the power of using Because Statements with your mantras and the importance of being very clear about what you want.

Her story also shows that by taking good notice of your phrases and messages and knowing they can be changed at any time, it helps you get that much closer every day to your ideal lifestyle.

You may continue reading or go to part two of this book and play with Mindware Experiment #10—Create Your Own Because Statement, as well as Mindware Experiment #11—Better Questions: The Sequel

CHAPTER 28

THE STORIES WE TELL

As you've discovered, most people spend the majority of their time on "automatic pilot." You might remember brain scientists estimate we spend 95% of our waking moments acting "unconsciously." You might also remember that 96% of the thoughts we have today are the same thoughts we had yesterday.

What you are learning with Train Your Brain is to live more "consciously", to become more "aware." As you do this, you will begin to reveal for yourself that many of the counter-productive thoughts you have today, are the same thoughts you had yesterday . . . and perhaps even the same as the thoughts you had a month ago or a year ago.

Part of the way these persistent ideas reveal themselves is in the stories we tell to ourselves and to the people around us. What do I mean by "stories?"

Think of stories as the dialog of your life. You share with others around you the day-to-day happenings in your life and these become your stories. You share your triumphs and your defeats. You share the good news, the bad news, and the boring news, and it all combines to become the story of your life.

And remember, what your repeatedly think about and talk about is stored in your unconscious mind as beliefs. Then the little matchmaker in your head spends all day every day matching the outside world picture to that inside world picture . . . that inner belief . . . that inner story.

Therefore, if you want your future to be different from your present, you must begin to tell new stories. When you start to tell a new story, you give your mind an opportunity to match a different inside world picture.

The incredible change that can occur by telling a new story is evidenced by this testimonial from one of my clients.

Several years ago, I was coaching someone who loved her home business and wanted to work it full time, but she was having a difficult time leaving her demanding day job.

I asked her what she did. She told me she'd been with a small mom and pop company for many years and felt very loyal to the owners.

I told her it was a nice story, so I asked, "Is there a problem?"

She immediately said to me,

> "There is no one else who can do what I do. No one has been able to learn my position and I would never leave the owners in a lurch. I want to work my home business full time, but my problem is I just don't see any way out."

Take a close look at her story. Was her "problem" that no one could learn her job position? No. The problem was the story she was telling.

I asked, "Is that really the story you want to tell?"

I explained that as long as she kept telling the same story over and over again, she would continue to find herself in the same situation over and over. And, unfortunately, because of this the likelihood of her finding a way out of that job would be slim.

Knowing this was an emotional dilemma for her, I gently asked if a sudden emergency prevented her from working, could the company go on without her? She agreed it could.

I said integrity and loyalty are great qualities and she should feel proud this was part of her makeup. I also suggested it was normal to feel the burden of leaving the owners in a lurch.

But more than anything, I wanted to drive home the point that she needed to tell a new stories. And the first person who should hear this new story was herself. After this, she could tell her "new story" to the owners if she so chose.

She agreed and began to tell a new story . . .

> "I don't have a ready answer to this situation right this
> minute, but I know that sometimes people can surprise us,
> and for all we know the person who will replace me could
> be right under our noses. Either way, I know that I am meant
> to work my home business full time and, if I keep my eyes
> open, the solution will present itself."

She continued telling her new story, first to herself, and then to everyone else who came into her life. In less than a month, she'd found someone in the company ready and able to take her position! Wow, huh?

After years and years of telling the same story, she finally found her way out simply by learning how to tell a new story.

Mantras, Transitory Statements, better questions, Because Statements, and telling a new story are ways to move your thoughts toward newer, more productive ways of thinking. They are also ways to remove self-defeating questions and counter-productive thinking.

You are uniquely wired, and that's why it's important to have as many options as possible to create your new outside picture of the world.

You may continue reading or go to part two of this book and play with Mindware Experiment #12—Tell A New Story

CHAPTER 29

BEYOND POSITIVE THINKING: THE EMOTIONAL SCALE

The positive thinking movement has been successful for many people and it has changed countless lives.

At the heart of the positive thinking movement is the idea that repeating positive phrases over and over—a method used to reprogram the unconscious mind—will ultimately "change" a person's habits or character traits.

Many people are convinced that words alone are producing the good results for them but, in fact, most of the time, it's emotion that's triggering change in the unconscious mind.

In other words, the most important building block for making change in the unconscious mind is emotion. So I'd like you to focus even more of your attention on emotion as a powerful tool for change.

At this point, you already have enough information and techniques from your Mindware Experiments to create dramatic change in your life and get your business booming quickly and effortlessly—and I've only touched on emotion. Now, I'm going to dig a bit deeper to show you the importance of emotion in catapulting your financial and personal success.

So far, I've talked about the magnitude of feeling good when you say your mantras. It's easy to tell someone to "feel good," right? But the reality is most of us are leading busy, complicated lives. We perform multiple roles. We manage many, many relationships. We have numerous obligations, deadlines, and other challenges. Stress has become a huge part of our lives.

So, how do we go about "feeling good" in any given moment?

Well, I'm going to spend this next section talking about The Emotional Scale and how to use it to feel good in any given moment.

There have been a variety of Emotional Scales floating around out there for quite some time. Maybe you've seen one with The Release Technique or one presented in the movie, The Secret. David Hawkins has a scale, which consists of more than a dozen levels and Abraham-Hicks's version of the scale has 22 levels.

The Train Your Brain version of the Emotional Scale is more simplified. And, although the general concept is the same, I've found that this simpler version is much easier to integrate into your daily life.

I've pulled some of the broad strokes from Abraham-Hicks' material on the Emotional Scale because they are proponents of so much good information in the personal development movement. If you don't know anything about Abraham-Hicks I highly recommend you check them out.

Here is the Train Your Brain version of The Emotional Scale and you will also find one for download at http://www.trainyourbrainformore.com,

THE EMOTIONAL SCALE

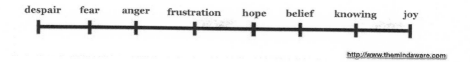

http://www.themindaware.com

As you can see, emotions run along a spectrum . . . with feelings of despair or depression on one end and feelings of bliss or joy on the other end. Between these two ends of the spectrum, emotions gradually feel "better" or "worse," depending which direction you move.

Most scales outline movement as up and down. I like the idea of moving side to side along the scale, for a couple of reasons:

First, my version of the Emotional Scale is a spectrum where emotions, like different colors of light, blend into one another and, thus, are not so rigidly defined. By making the scale less defined, I believe movement along the scale is far easier.

I also think by having an Emotional Scale that defines movement as up or down suggests moving up equals "good" and moving down is somehow "bad" or "negative." On a day-to-day basis our emotions are always "in motion," and you will soon learn that benefit can be gained from all emotions on the scale.

At one end of the Emotional Scale, you find despair or depression, often characterized as a feeling of powerlessness. Sometimes these feelings can make something as simple as getting out of bed difficult. For most, this sense of powerlessness takes place in mere moments or in certain areas of their lives. For others, it can feel like an overarching kind of metaphorical darkness, which leaves a knot in their stomachs.

One spot over from despair is fear or worry. These emotions feel similar to powerlessness, but they are typically characterized by the sense of some kind of impending doom or disaster. People experiencing these feelings often worry about aspects of their lives they feel they can't control, and they fear the worst outcome.

Moving over on the scale from fear is anger. Sometimes anger can feel like revenge. With this feeling you might experience moving away from powerlessness by "taking back your power." But I'm not talking about anger that's misplaced or physically threatening, or destructive; I'm speaking of anger as a more "active" emotion than, say, despair or fear, which are typically "passive" in nature.

Granted, anger might not be the most constructive use of your power, but at least anger feels like you are actually doing something. This feeling of "accomplishment" generated by a bit of good, healthy anger, however small, can be just enough to keep someone moving along the scale.

Next spot on the scale is frustration. More "tame" than anger, frustration may feel like annoyance or being overwhelmed or too busy. The smallest things become magnified and tiny obstacles become insurmountable roadblocks.

After frustration comes hope. This is the first feeling along the scale I would call "productive." It is characterized by a feeling of optimism . . . by the simple thought that your life isn't certain to turn out well, but there's a good chance it might. The feeling of hope sometimes feels like "wishing."

After hope is belief. Belief is a stronger feeling than hope and is characterized by a sense of positive expectation or anticipating a good outcome with confidence. The general feeling behind belief is that getting what one wants or desires is a "strong realistic possibility."

One spot over on the scale after belief comes the feeling of knowing. Characterized by a sense of complete confidence, certainty, or assuredness, knowing is an interesting place on the Emotional Scale— and I'll talk more about knowing later.

Finally, on the far end of the Emotional Scale is the feeling of joy. Some call this feeling of elevated happiness, bliss, or being in a state of appreciation. Every time we have a huge belly laugh, we're in a state of joy. Or maybe it's the rush of feeling we get when we look at our spouse or partner or child or friend with appreciation and happiness.

There you have it. That's the Train Your Brain Emotional Scale.

All your feelings fall somewhere along this Emotional Scale. Everything you experience with regards to "how you feel" runs along this spectrum of emotion. And, as you move along the scale, each emotion you experience feels just a bit better or worse, depending on the direction you're moving.

As you become more familiar with The Emotional Scale, you'll see how movement along the scale doesn't require you to make huge leaps. No matter how insignificant they might seem to you, these smaller movements will still have a dramatic and powerful impact on your life and create positive results for your business. You will learn as we continue, the whole key here is movement and "moving one step" at a time along the scale is important. You will get off of the "roller coaster ride" of emotions.

As you learn how to use the Emotional Scale, you may feel an emotion that's not listed. You might want to place that particular feeling on the scale. For example, if you feel "anxious," ask yourself, "Is this feeling of anxiety similar to the feeling of fear, or is it more like a feeling of excitement?" You'll soon see, with practice, you can use broad strokes and place yourself on the scale for any emotion you feel.

Remember, everything you do depends almost entirely on emotion and you will learn how to use the Emotional Scale to navigate your way through your countless feelings.

CHAPTER 30

HOW SHOULD I FEEL TODAY

You will be digging deeper into the Emotional Scale, but first, a good old-fashioned story which really shows how often we're "held captive" by the external circumstances happening in the world around us.

This is a parable common in Eastern spiritual philosophy and has been told several different ways. I'm going to tell you my favorite version.

Once upon a time in a small village, there was a man who had a son and a pony. These were the two things in life he loved the most, and so he was a happy man.

One day, the pony ran away. No one in the village could find the pony anywhere and the man became quite saddened. He thought to himself, "how can I go on living without my pony?" The man was clearly despondent.

After several days without word of the pony's whereabouts, the pony finally returned to the village, bringing with him, a beautiful Arabian horse. The man was so happy! "My beloved pony is back and now I also have a beautiful Arabian horse," he exclaimed. The man was overjoyed by this sudden turn of events.

A few days later, his son attempted to ride the horse. He succeeded for a while but, while galloping at a good pace, the boy fell off and broke his leg. The man was immediately saddened by this unfortunate accident and, believing such a tragic thing would never strike his own boy, the man cried loudly, "He will be lame!" The man was so very sad.

Several days later, the military came into the village and declared they would be taking away all able-bodied men in order to help fight the war. Many young men left their families, and some were never seen again. But because this man's son had a broken leg, the boy was spared. The old man was relieved and jubilant.

So what's the end of the story? The end of the story is, there is no end.

The moral of the story is the man will continue walking through life always at the mercy of outside circumstances. He will continually look to the world around him for outside evidence; feeling good or feeling bad will be based exclusively on any random event or circumstances that come his way. And he will depend on these external cues to tell him how he should feel on any given day.

This man will never know true happiness because his feelings will always be dictated by things he can't control.

The REASON I tell this story is because, unfortunately, many people are running their businesses in this same way.

Those just starting out may design their business card and become extremely excited about their business. Then, as they start to talk with people about their new business, they get a few rejections and they quickly become discouraged.

Then a few days later, they may meet someone who buys their product or books an appointment and they're happy once again. But then, the next day they have a product returned or a cancellation and next thing you know, they're frustrated again.

Then they might attend a live motivational seminar and leave feeling confident, recharged and positive. But after several financial disappointments over the coming weeks, they feel down again.

The events are quite common for entrepreneurs trying to get their businesses off the ground; but the "roller-coaster" of emotion arising from these events comes down to a lack of "intentional thinking."

A lack of "intentional thinking" is when, like the man in our parable, you're simply looking for cues or waiting to react to the various events in your life rather than being proactive and generating or "producing" thoughts from within which create positive emotion.

This is acting like a puppet on a string, letting whatever circumstances come along pull the strings and dictate how you think and feel.

By merely reacting to events rather than taking the initiative with more proactive thinking, your thoughts and emotions will ALWAYS mirror what's happening around you.

Subsequently, if the events in your life are random, inconsistent and unpredictable, then your thoughts and emotions will ALWAYS be random, inconsistent and unpredictable.

When you let the uncontrollable determine if you feel good, or doubtful, or frustrated, or hopeful, you will continually swing back and forth on the Emotional Scale. You will also see little progress and change in your business.

In addition, if you continue allowing external circumstances to dictate how you feel, you'll always be at the mercy of the situations in your life that are completely beyond your control.

So you really want to use more "intentional thinking" by trying to take control of your own thoughts and emotions rather than automatically reacting to every random event coming into your life.

Training Your Brain means you'll never fall into the trap of depending on external circumstances to rule your life and business. You won't yo-yo back and forth on the scale and when you do slide back from time to time, you have the proper tools and knowledge to "right the ship." You'll get back to ruling your own life and your business much quicker than you have been able to do in the past! How exciting is that?

Train Your Brain helps you to get your mind "aware" of how dependent you can be on outside circumstances and how much these circumstances can rule your life. But Train Your Brain's true effectiveness comes from getting you back in control of your own thoughts so you can generate your own good feelings and realize success will happen for you regardless of external happenings.

All this makes a more stable foundation from which to build your own strong and financially—thriving business. And you'll know you don't need to ride a roller-coaster to success or Ping-Pong back and forth along the Emotional Scale. You will see dramatic and positive shifts in your business simply by taking control of your thoughts and emotions.

CHAPTER 31

ARE BAD EMOTIONS BAD?

Talking about human feelings, noted psychiatrist and influential thinker Carl Jung said,

....

"There can be no transforming of
darkness into light and of apathy into
movement without emotion."

....

Throughout the rest of this book, I'm going to show you how counter-productive or negative emotions influence you and how your own feelings become warning signals for change.

I'll piece together the concepts of the conscious mind, the unconscious mind and emotion in a brand new way to show you how to make change in any area of your life quickly and effortlessly.

However, first I want to address a common misconception that negative or counter-productive emotions are "bad".

As you've learned, thoughts create your feelings and beliefs, and your beliefs create your outside pictures of the world. With this knowledge, a pervasive theme that has taken hold in today's culture is that negative thoughts are sabotaging our success.

The suggestion you are somehow sabotaging your own chance for success and happiness is thoroughly self-defeating. By equating so-called negative emotions with failure, experts are effectively blaming people for experiencing less-than positive feelings.

This makes most people afraid to acknowledge their counter-productive feelings. That also forces some to deny their negative emotions entirely. This repressive approach to emotions, and the unfortunate blame-game which naturally follows, creates a clear and damaging message that negative emotions are "bad."

Well, I'd like to tell you right now, the opposite is true. Negative emotions are not bad, and they certainly won't sabotage your chance for success. Not only are negative emotions necessary, they're also useful.

With Train Your Brain, you will start to realize all emotions, good and bad, are part of the full spectrum of what makes us human. You will learn that being able to identify your negative emotions helps you to understand what you DO want in life and you will learn how to use this information to your own advantage.

Acceptance of your "negative" emotions makes you a lot more aware of your positive feelings and also gives you the best chance for real movement along the Emotional Scale.

I'm sure you've heard the old adage, "You can't appreciate the sun unless you've experienced rain!" Because of negative emotions, we know what positive emotions are and what they mean to us.

Recognize and accept all your emotions—"good ones" and "bad ones"—as both necessary and useful. This helps you know where you are on the Emotional Scale more quickly and will get you moving in the right direction much sooner. Why?

Because knowing where you are on the scale, which is simply your acceptance of a feeling, even if it is a negative one, creates movement. As a result, you won't be afraid to acknowledge feelings deemed "negative" by others.

My motto about any kind of emotion: Acknowledge it. Embrace it. Use it. This is how we make change . . . and it's certainly better than beating yourself up, don't you think?

When you know what you are feeling at any given time, you are able to place that emotion on the Emotional Scale. When you can place that emotion on the Emotional Scale, you now have the opportunity for movement along the scale and you are able to move to any other emotion on that scale.

The simplest and most effective way to manage your own feelings, especially those that may be a bit self-defeating, is to bring that feeling of anger, frustration or doubt into your conscious awareness.

This more proactive approach—emotional awareness—happens when you hold your feelings up to the light. You are then able to see how different your many feelings are not better, not worse, just different.

Look at emotional awareness as a kind of daily ritual by consistently taking stock of your feelings no matter what the situation may be. You'll develop an attitude that forgetting, banishing, repressing, or even blaming yourself for your negative or counter-productive feelings has no place in your vision or desire to build a highly successful business.

Managing emotions can be challenging without the proper tools. Of course you want feel good all the time, but to do so would deny what makes you human. Your emotions are constantly fluctuating and so make a clear choice to recognize and accept each of your feelings, "good" and "bad." If you do so, you won't be trying to "fix" how you think or how you feel.

Now that you're becoming more emotionally aware, you will know where you are on the Emotional Scale more consistently. As a result, you will have a much clearer picture of yourself. You'll find yourself moving along the scale more quickly and effortlessly. And you'll finally see how decisions and choices which seemed so difficult in the past become easier, almost second nature, now that you understand the impact of emotional awareness.

By learning how to effectively navigate your way through your complex feelings, you've created a nice little shortcut for yourself; because until you know where you are on the Emotional Scale—whether you're feeling angry, frustrated, hopeful, or blissful—you can't move.

CHAPTER 32

FEELINGS AS SIGNALS

If you have been conducting your Mindware Experiments, I hope it's becoming clear that your feelings don't magically rise up inside you. There is rhyme and reason for every single feeling you experience and understanding your feelings is easily accomplished through emotional awareness.

The fact is, all your emotions are generated by simple, conscious thoughts in the brain—and up until now, these thoughts have been just reactions to the external circumstances, or outside evidence, in your life.

So as you strengthen your emotional awareness, you will begin to look at your feelings as "signals" or clues that alert you to pay attention to your thoughts.

As I said before, the only way to manage your countless feelings is to take notice of your thoughts. Train Your Brain isn't built on a whole set of rules etched in stone, but if there is one rule that comes close it's this:

....

What you think creates how you feel.

....

In other words, what you are feeling at any given moment is the most important clue to what you're thinking at that very same moment. The emotion you are feeling is your "signal."

Most often we think of feelings as "emotional states" or "mental sensations", but when we think of emotions as "signals," it helps to counteract some of those cultural feelings that certain emotions are "bad."

In addition, in thinking of our feelings as "signals" we're able to draw some parallels to other bodily sensations with which we're more familiar.

For example, "feelings" also occur as part of the nervous system in the body. Each of us has nerve endings or receptors on our skin, which respond to physical pain or tactile feelings of pleasure. "Feelings" or "sensations" take place when a part of the body perceives or responds to physical sensations like pain or pleasure and these feelings are then transmitted as messages to the brain.

So if you hold your hand over a burning candle and you experience physical pain, you quickly remove your hand from the candle unless you want to burn yourself.

The physical sensation of pain picked up by the pain receptors instantly generates a thought in the brain, which perceives this pain by saying, "Ouch! That hurts!"

Simultaneously, another thought in the brain says, "Move your hand away from the candle to stop the pain!"

So, naturally you pay attention to this important pain signal and respond almost automatically, seemingly without thinking, by removing your hand from the flame.

This is a no-brainer, right?

It is. So why, then, don't we respond in such a "matter-of-fact" manner when dealing with emotional feelings as signals? It's funny, isn't it?

If you were holding your hand over a burning flame it would never occur to you to think, "What's the matter with me for feeling pain?" or "Why can't I get myself to stop feeling pain?" or "Wouldn't it be great to have no sensation of pain?"

Isn't it strange that we often criticize ourselves in exactly this way for having negative emotions? We ask ourselves, "What's the matter with me? Why can't I just be positive? Why do I have to feel pain?"

Your emotional feelings are also warning signs similar to the signal of physical pain from a burning flame.

The pain you feel from the burning flame indicates to your brain that you need to move your hand. And when you feel emotional pain, it's an indication to your brain that you need to move your thoughts.

The point is, if you look at your feelings as "signals" and respond with the same matter-of-fact urgency as you would a burning flame, you wouldn't eliminate feelings that make you feel bad. You'd realize that sensations of pain are useful indicators of the steps you need to take to feel better.

That's what Train Your Brain teaches you . . . by keeping a watchful eye on your "negative" emotions, you'll see your feelings as necessary and useful, and as important signals to move away from counter-productive emotions much quicker than in the past, and not because you've repressed or banished these feelings.

We all know it's natural for our bodies to want to feel better when we're not feeling good; it's why we move our hand away from a burning flame when it's painful.

Think about how many times we have a sniffle or a tickle in our throat and quickly see this as a sign we're getting sick.

So <u>what</u> do we do?

We do everything we can do to start feeling better. We blast ourselves with vitamin C, rest, or various cold remedies.

So <u>why</u> do we do this?

We're listening to our body's "signal" and responding without much thought. Because we've been told feeling physically sick is a natural part of life and there are countless things we can do to help ourselves feel better, that's exactly what we do.

Well, your emotions, even the not-so-good ones, are also natural. And "wanting to feel better" is a natural reaction when you're feeling doubtful, frustrated, or angry.

So strengthen your emotional awareness by first looking at your feelings as "signals," and then zooming in on your thoughts. That helps you respond more "automatically" when you're feeling discouraged or angry or uncertain.

Paying closer attention to your thoughts by continually tuning into your signals—a burning flame, a scratchy throat, a touch of anger or some self-doubt—you'll begin to see the world around you soften a bit. You'll see that what "happens" to you is far less important than what you "make happen."

Your feelings should never be banished, repressed, gotten rid of or buried. All your feelings, positive and negative, are equally important, and are signals telling you what you are thinking. And, simply by changing your line of thinking—because thoughts create all your emotions—you can get yourself feeling better with ease.

Remember, what you think is how you feel.

In these final Mindware Experiments, you'll review everything you've learned up until now about your thoughts and emotions and how they relate to the Emotional Scale, and begin applying it directly to your business.

You'll discover how you can get your emotions and thoughts working in harmony. You'll learn how you can spend more time in hope and belief and knowing and joy, the more "productive" places on the Emotional Scale.

You'll also learn how simple it is to be less influenced by outside circumstances in your life and how, by practicing a few easy-to-learn techniques in your business, you can generate more of your own thoughts—independent of outside influence—to create powerful and successful shifts in your business and your life.

CHAPTER 33

Emotions in Motion

As was mentioned earlier, many times your movement along the Emotional Scale results from an event, situation, or external circumstance. You may see or hear something you like or don't like and have certain reactions in the form of conscious thoughts which immediately trigger an emotion or feeling.

You've also discovered that thoughts always create emotion. This means if you want to experience a "different feeling" from an emotion you are experiencing, you must intentionally think different thoughts to "move" yourself to a different place on the Emotional Scale.

In addition, you've learned that each emotion on the Emotional Scale feels one notch better or one notch worse, depending on the direction.

Well, one additional piece of information, which you will find useful, is that it's most easy and natural to move along the Emotional Scale one step at a time. In fact, this is how the scale works . . . if you want to intentionally move yourself to a more positive emotional place, then you MUST do it one step at a time.

You can't make leaps in feeling and go from anger to bliss or from fear to knowing without kidding yourself. Your brain is naturally wired to move one step at a time along the scale.

Have you ever had the experience of being in a bad mood or worrying about something and then some really perky positive thinker comes up to you and says, "You should think more positive and appreciative because you know you bring about what you think about!" Well, when that happens, it doesn't help you to feel positive, does it? If anything, it probably makes you angry, right? Why does this make you angry? Because, if you take a close look at the scale, appreciation is very, very far away from fear and worry. It's WAY too big of a jump on the Emotional Scale to go from worry to appreciation. On the other hand, if you look at the scale you're also going to see that anger is right next door to fear and worry and so when you're feeling worried, being angry is quite easy to access.

So we take this knowledge about the Emotional Scale and we use it to our advantage. If we can only move one step at a time along the Emotional Scale, then let's intentionally move ourselves emotionally along the scale.

What I mean is this . . .

Let's say you are feeling fear or worry about something related to your business and you'd give anything to feel more hopeful about the particular situation. In order for you to move from fear or worry towards a more hopeful feeling, you MUST, and I mean MUST, pass through the other emotions on the scale first. In other words, moving appropriately along the scale means you need to first feel anger and then you need to feel frustration and then you get to feelings of hope.

So how do you "make" yourself feel certain emotions?

There is only one way and that's by using your own brain . . . by using your own THOUGHTS.

And so, if you are feeling worried, and you want to move toward feeling hopeful, you start out by trying to get yourself to feel angry . . . and you do that by purposefully . . . by intentionally thinking angry thoughts. Start thinking thoughts like, "Boy, people are stupid! Why can't they just see that I've got the best products and service on the planet! They're all making me crazy!" Keep saying sentences like this until you actually FEEL angry.

Now it probably goes without saying that you don't want to stay in this place emotionally. In other words, you don't want to stay steeped in anger. You want to purposely, intentionally feel angry, but only for a few minutes. It really doesn't take any longer than this. After feeling anger for a short while, you then want to look to the next spot on the Emotional Scale and move to that emotional place. So your next stop is . . . frustration! And to get yourself to feeling frustrated . . . you'll want to intentionally think thoughts that sound like frustration like, "I feel like I'm working hard and nothing seems to be sticking. I just find the whole situation a little annoying. I'm feeling pretty frustrated with the whole thing."

Again, only stay in this emotional place, frustration, for a few minutes . . . until it feels natural and then start to intentionally and deliberately think thoughts, which make you feel hopeful. They could be thoughts like, "I hope I start to feel better. I hope I think of a solution. I hope I get a new customer today. I hope one of my old clients calls with an order. I hope I start to feel more hopeful. I hope my business grows faster this year."

You can say these sentences to yourself or you can say them out loud, but keep saying them until you can actually FEEL the emotional shift in your body. Keep saying these hopeful sentences until you actually feel hopeful.

If you keep saying them beyond that point, you'll find yourself automatically moving into even higher levels on the Emotional Scale. Meaning, if you keep saying "hopeful" statements, you'll automatically start saying statements that start with "I believe" and other emotions even further on the scale. Your positive thoughts will just move you along. Even better, just keep intentionally "choosing" thoughts that move you into belief and then knowing and then joy.

However, there is one other very important point about hope:

. . . .

If you can consistently feel more
hopeful about your business, this is all
you need to become successful.

. . . .

If you get to hope on the Emotional Scale, you will feel a sense of success. In fact, hope can carry you a long way toward creating positive change for yourself, and is actually "enough" for many, many people.

In other words, you don't need to be steeped in bliss and joy every day for your business to be successful. If you're only able to move yourself to the levels of hope or belief on a regular basis . . . this is enough. You can take action in your business from these two emotional places and you will see good results. The point is, don't think you need to feel joyful or blissful to be successful in your business. Even if you simply make a concentrated and deliberate effort to get to hope on the Emotional Scale you will not only have access to more creative and inventive thinking you will, in turn, grow your business as well.

Here's a quick exercise, which shows you how certain thoughts can change how you feel.

During this exercise, you'll be reading to yourself or, if you're in a place where you can read these words out loud, go ahead, whatever works best for you.

You'll be reading and describing certain thoughts someone might have about themselves and their surroundings while running a typical small business. Then you'll "overlay" these thoughts with a corresponding feeling from the Emotional Scale.

This is an experiment, so it's not important to identify with every feeling you'll be describing. It's more important to be aware of your own feelings and notice of how dependent emotion is on your particular thoughts as you read.

You'll be starting on one end of the Emotional Scale in despair and eventually be working your way to the other end of the scale to joy or appreciation. I want you to relax and take note of your feelings as you read the words. As you move along the Emotional Scale, see if your feelings change as your thoughts change.

Okay. Let's begin.

Again, you will start out on the far left-hand side of the Emotional Scale where despair is the prevailing feeling:

Read and think . . . "I really made a mistake trying to convince myself I could do this business. I can't imagine being able to make a go of it. I don't even want to talk with people about the business. It's not going to work. Can't anyone see that? Can't anyone see there's nothing I can do to change it? It's not realistic at all anymore. What a waste! I made a huge mistake."

Take note of your feelings and keep relaxing.

Okay. Let's move on. You want to feel better and so you intentionally think thoughts that sound like fear.

Read and think . . . "If I keep trying to talk to people, I'm afraid they'll think I'm pushy. I don't want to be rejected. I've invested so much time and money into this business, I'm worried I'll never be able to recoup my investment. I'm just scared I may have to quit."

Stay aware of how you're feeling and keep on relaxing.

Okay. Let's keep moving. You want to feel better and so you intentionally think thoughts that sound like anger.

Read and think . . . "Everyone is driving me crazy! I have great products and services and no one seems to get that! It just really pisses me off! What's the matter with people . . . and what's the matter with me? I see other people who are successful. Why can't it happen for me? I'm trying so hard! I just can't believe it's not working!"

Keep aware of how easily your feelings are changing and stay relaxed . . . you're going to move again.

Okay. Let's keep moving. You want to feel better and so you intentionally think thoughts that sound like frustration.

Read and think . . . "Sometimes it feels like it's one step forward and two steps backwards in this business. I can't seem to get any forward momentum and it's annoying. I'm just not getting enough response. I want more. Sometimes things are good and sometimes slow. It's so frustrating! And I don't know how to fix it. I wish I could figure out what I'm doing wrong."

Notice the changes in feeling . . . stay relaxed . . . you're moving again.

Okay. Let's keep moving. You want to feel better and so you intentionally think thoughts that sound like hope.

Read and think . . . "Any person who has ever been successful in any business started in exactly the same place I'm in right now. I've learned other things in the past, and this is just another thing to learn. I'm hopeful I can just hang in there and take baby steps. Small steps every day is how others have made it work and I'm hopeful I'll find a way to make it work for me too. I'm hopeful something will break for me soon."

Notice how seamless the transition is from frustration to hope just by changing your thoughts. Stay relaxed . . . that's right, you're on the move once again.

You want to feel better and so you intentionally think thoughts that sound like belief.

Read and think . . . "This is really starting to work. Everything is falling into place and I can see my business starting to come along. I can see there is such a need for the product and service I'm providing to others. There is so much good potential with this business and I believe my efforts are paying off. And the best part is, I'm starting to FEEL successful. I'm in the right place at the right time and I'm just going to ride this wave!"

Notice the changes in feeling . . . stay relaxed . . . you're moving again.

Your feeling of belief is getting stronger. Now you expect to be successful. In fact, you KNOW you'll be successful no matter what.

You want to feel better and so you intentionally think thoughts that sound like knowing.

Read and think . . . "I know this is going to work. It's almost effortless now. I can feel it in every fiber of my body that I was meant to do this. I am so excited about my products and services. I love working for myself and I love helping people. Everything is going my way and I'm looking forward to just watching it all unfold!"

Wow, right? Did you feel that incredible rush of feeling? Can you see how easily a few simple thoughts can make you feel so much better?

Okay . . . stay relaxed . . . you have one more move.

You want to feel better and so you intentionally think thoughts that sound like joy.

Read and think . . . "I am so thankful to be walking this path and doing this business. I am so grateful that I know how to keep my thoughts in alignment with my dreams and I can see that all of my small steps are leading in the right direction. I love my business!! I'm so happy and thankful that I am on this path and I am ready!"

Okay. That's it!

Did you notice your feelings actually changing as you read the words? Did you also notice that it didn't take you very long to cover the entire spectrum and to move your feelings from despair to joy? By the time you were done, weren't you feeling excited about running a business?

Studying the Emotional Scale and learning the various thoughts, which correspond with each place on the scale, will help you immensely as you conduct the upcoming Mindware Experiment.

This main point is you're going to be creating thoughts on your own, and thinking independently of outside influence, and you don't even have to "believe" what you're saying! From the moment you sound these words off in your head, these "new thoughts" will generate new feelings and you will find yourself moving much quicker along the Emotional Scale.

You may continue reading or go to part two of this book and play with Mindware Experiment #13—Travelling The Emotional Scale

CHAPTER 34

THE POWER OF KNOWING

Of all of the emotions on the Emotional Scale, perhaps "knowing" is the most elusive. For most of us, a general understanding of what a specific feeling means to us holds true for all the other emotions on the Emotional Scale.

If someone asked if you've ever felt depressed or powerless, you'd probably say, "Oh sure." How about worried? "You bet." How about frustrated, or angry, or hopeful? "Yes, yes, and yes."

Even the feeling of belief seems easy to grasp, because it's so often used as a term to express ideas, such as "I believe in the general good of people." "I believe his intentions were to do the right thing" or even, "I believe in Santa Claus."

And of course you probably feel appreciation on some level every day or at least each time you say, "thank you."

But what really is this feeling of knowing?

When I do live trainings, I get questions on the topic of knowing more than any other feeling on the Emotional Scale. So I'd like to explain my own sense of knowing.

In its simplest definition, a feeling of knowing is a sense of certainty or assuredness. Perhaps encompassing a sensation a bit more "in your body," knowing doesn't just occupy your mind. It seems to go beyond words.

Sometimes knowing can be likened to a feeling of faith, spiritual or otherwise; a strong belief something is going to happen without any "evidence" it's going to happen. You just know.

Knowing can appear as intuition. You might say, "I knew that was going to happen" or "I knew there was something funny about that guy." Then someone will immediately ask you, "How did you know?" And you'll answer, "I'm not really sure how I knew. I just knew.

Knowing also appears when you've garnered enough life experience and knowledge about yourself, your business, and your life, to know without a shadow of a doubt who you are and where you are going.

And of course, the feeling of "knowing" occurs as you become more aware of your own thoughts and make the connection between how you think and the circumstances in your own life.

All of this is "knowing" or at the very least, pieces of it.

As I said earlier, the feeling of "knowing" is a bit different than typical emotions on the scale. It is harder to define in concrete terms and language, but it may help to begin by seeing knowing as the culmination of everything you've learned along the way.

And while it may even seem like a big payoff, to be in a place of knowing, in upcoming Mindware Experiments we'll explore the idea that you probably are already in a place of "knowing" in many, many areas of your life. And understanding this feeling of knowing in certain areas of your life will help you to cultivate it in other areas as well.

CHAPTER 35

KNOWING IN ACTION

I had a discussion with someone recently. She was trying to attain a financial goal. She wanted to earn $30,000 a month in her business. At the time she made the goal, she was only earning just over $10,000 a month and so it was a huge stretch for her to reach this new level.

She had been working for the goal for well over a year and over the previous few months she had finally reached the point where she was consistently earning $27,000-$29,000 a month.

When she met with me, I expected her to want to talk about how to close the gap on that last few thousand dollars and actually hit her goal of $30,000 a month, but much to my surprise, she actually wanted to talk about attaining the $50,000 level.

Out of curiosity, I asked her why she didn't want to talk about her original $30,000 goal. In my mind, I knew she hadn't actually attained that goal yet, and so I was curious as to what she was thinking. When I asked, she said, "Well, I know I'm going to hit it. It's just a matter of time and so I want to start laying the groundwork for the next level."

I thought about what she said . . . "I KNOW I'm going to hit it." Her answer gave me some insight into the feeling of "knowing." If I had asked if she KNEW she was going to hit that goal one year earlier when she was at the $10,000 level, she would have probably answered that she was hopeful, but she didn't "know" it. So what had changed?

What had changed was her experience. She had taken a lot of baby steps toward her goal, which had met with success and helped to build her confidence. She kept creeping toward her goal to the point where she now knew she would still be able to creep just a little further.

She had the experience behind her to "know" that she could make the last few thousand on her own, without my guidance. So when she met with me, she wanted to talk about the new goal, which at this point seemed like a hopeful dream and not the goal that she "knew" she would attain.

She "knew" she would attain her original goal because she had been "building a case" for her success.

After talking with her, I realized that this feeling of "knowing" was something I had leveraged for myself when building my million dollar business in direct sales.

As I mentioned earlier, sometimes this "state of knowing" simply results when we gather evidence from our past experiences. I had enough evidence from my past life experiences to "know" that I could accomplish the tasks I needed to accomplish in order to be successful in my direct sales business.

I had learned how to develop other skills in my life and I was sure I could learn this skill too. I knew the company had processes and systems in place to help me succeed and I was sure I could take advantage of their training. I also knew that others had walked before me and been successful in this same type of business and so why wouldn't it work for me too?

With each small task that came my way in my business, I asked myself a few questions:

1. Could I trust in the process or system? Was there a certain process, method, or technique that I knew worked for other people? Even if I didn't have self-confidence in a certain area, I could trust that the process was sound and it would work if I applied it to my business.

2. Had others done it successfully? Had others accomplished what I wanted to accomplish? Was it possible? Did other people possess some special talent or magical power or did they just learn certain skills, which helped them accomplish certain tasks at hand, because if they could learn those skills, then I could learn those skills.

And with each small success I gained more evidence and more confidence that it would work. I didn't start out in the beginning "knowing" that I would reach the million dollar level in 19 months, but I did start out "knowing" that I could learn everything I needed to know to be successful and I knew I was willing to implement that education.

In hindsight I also know now that this sense of "knowing" made my rise easier. The feeling of "knowing" carried with it the same sense of relief people have when they talk about "faith"—the faith that things will turn out well.

The point is that you are probably in the same state of knowing in a variety of areas in your own life. Areas where you've had enough past experience that, often, you feel pretty certain of what will "happen" next.

Think about all the things you've understood . . . mastered . . . accomplished . . . pulled off . . . brought about . . . taken care of . . .

proudly executed . . . managed or carried out . . . the things you've completed . . . the things you didn't give up on . . . all your feats, talents, skills . . . and your triumphs . . . all of this is "good evidence."

Think of your own good evidence. Remember a time when you were first learning something. Do you remember how nervous you were about accomplishing it? Maybe it was giving a presentation for the first time or the first time you talked to someone about your product or service.

Over time you practice and learn and you gain confidence about your products and your services. And there comes a point when you can't imagine NOT being confident at your offerings! You've already had many, many successes in your business. Take a moment to feel that sense of achievement from all that you have learned and taken on and succeeded at in your business.

You may continue reading or go to part two of this book and play with Mindware Experiment #14—What Is Knowing, as well as Mindware Experiment #15—Beyond Belief and Mindware Experiment #16— The Hope Exercise.

CHAPTER 36

INTENTIONAL ACTION

Many years ago, when I was first presenting Train Your Brain to live audiences, a man who had studied a lot of motivational material told me what he liked best about my training was the section on Intentional Action.

I asked him why and he said, "With other training I always felt like I was being told to just sit around, think happy thoughts, and good things would just fall into my lap."

He said Intentional Action helps put people in control and be more proactive about their lives, rather than "waiting around" for motivation.

If you've followed the self-help and inspirational movements, you're probably familiar with the term "inspired action." It can be loosely defined as a means of making known your desires, dreams, and goals and then listening to your intuition or "inner voice" which will tell you what action to take.

The challenge with "inspired action" is that it sometimes does feel as if you're not doing much. And often, if you do get a "feeling" to take some type of action, you're still left wondering, "Was I 'inspired' to do this?"

So, for me, Intentional Action made more sense.

Intentional Action is any action you take after you've made an "intentional and conscious" effort to move yourself to an emotionally positive place.

In other words . . .

Only AFTER you've intentionally moved yourself to a more emotionally positive place using your own thoughts do you ever take ANY action in your business.

You don't sit around and wait for that inspirational nudge or inner voice telling you when you can act. You use intentionally "think better thoughts"—which is an act in itself—to create "better" feelings. Then when you take action, any action you take is the right action!

This is Intentional Action.

Every so often I will talk with someone who says, "I'm feeling really down. Nothing is working for me and so I'm thinking I should just make a bunch of calls to potential customers to see if I can drum something up."

At which point I would immediately say, "Please don't," and here is why . . .

When you attempt to carry out any business-related or action-oriented tasks from a place of powerlessness, hopelessness, frustration, or anger, these actions will turn out poorly.

Simply put, "actions" performed from these places on the Emotional Scale are doomed to disaster from the start.

So if you're experiencing any kind of counter-productive feelings, do NOTHING. Do not take any "action" to try to move your business forward. The ONLY thing you should be "doing" is taking steps to make yourself feel better. The very first step to take in your business is to move your emotions forward.

Apply all you've been learning in Train Your Brain. Choose thoughts that help you move to the next, more positive place on the Emotional Scale.

I always tell clients who are convinced doing anything is better than feeling frustrated about their businesses, "Please don't. Do nothing. Do the Hope Exercise or some other Train Your Brain exercise. Get yourself feeling better, even if that's all you 'do' for a couple of days."

And time and time again, I would hear from them within a couple of days and they would say something like, "You'll never guess what happened to me? Someone walked up to me in a gas station yesterday and booked an appointment!"

Or, another might say, "I had this fantastic marketing idea! It's like it came out of the blue!"

But of course, it didn't come out of the blue. As you know by now, when you move yourself to an emotionally positive place, you have a more resourceful and creative mind. Ideas occur to you that were not available when you were feeling "stuck." In addition, you give off a positive "aura." People want to approach you!

At The Mind Aware we have countless stories of clients who have benefited from "taking action" AFTER feeling better about their business.

So the "act" of doing nothing, does not hurt anyone's business. In fact, instead of fighting negative feelings, you'll get much better results by doing nothing at first, using your own thoughts to move yourself in a "more positive direction" along the Emotional Scale . . . and THEN taking action.

When you do that, good, positive results follow.

You may continue reading or go to part two of this book and play with Mindware Experiment #17—Change Your Breathing, as well as Mindware Experiment #18—Change Your Body Language

CHAPTER 37

HOW ANYONE GETS ANYWHERE

So how does anyone get anywhere? If you're going to Oregon, do you really need to figure out where you were yesterday to get there? Not really. You just start from where you are.

This section is adapted from material I learned from Bill Harris at the Centerpointe Research Institute. It further illustrates the important connection between thought, emotion, and action, and ultimately led to my concept of Intentional Action.

No matter what the outcome you intend or desire, there are six important steps to getting anywhere:

1. Know where you are.
2. Know where you want to go.
3. Take action.
4. Evaluate the results of your action.
5. Refine the action.
6. Repeat steps 3, 4, and 5 . . . until you get where you want to go.

Let's look at each step in more detail.

STEP 1: KNOW WHERE YOU ARE

Begin evaluating the circumstances of your situation honestly, without judgment or blame or beating yourself up for where you are. You just know where you are. And whether this appears good or bad to you, this is where you start.

Again, don't spend time evaluating how you got where you are. You don't need reasons or excuses for why you're here; regrets will bog you down.

This step takes one or two minutes. Begin by saying to yourself something such as, "I'm an entrepreneur who does $10,000 in retail sales each month" or, "I'm a small business owner with 20 clients" or anything equally simple, and honest.

The point is, you need to know where you are in order to determine where you want to go.

STEP 2: KNOW WHERE YOU WANT TO GO

Often people make far too big a deal with this step. It is important in the overall process, but you needn't spend a ton of time on where you want to go.

However, having said that, if you just say, "I want to go somewhere," that's not enough information to know what action to take to get you where you want to go. It's vague and wishy-washy. So, it is important to have a clear destination point.

With the Oregon example, saying, "I want to go west," at least tells you which direction you intend to go, but where is west, really? And how would you know when you got there?

How about, "I'm going to Portland, Oregon?" Isn't it better if you're trying to be more specific about where you want to go?

So as you look more closely at your business, the more specific you are about where you want to go, the more you'll know how to start and how to determine if you're moving toward your destination.

However, while it's important to be specific, it's always far more important to feel good. In other words, being more specific should never squash or diminish your good feelings about where you want to go.

So in this second step, if specific details feel a bit overwhelming or if any other negative feeling begins to emerge for you, simply broaden your vision a bit. This will reduce the stress about where you want to go.

Here's an example of "broadening your vision." You can first start specific:

> Step 1: Know Where You Are
> Where am I?—"I'm a small business owner with 20 clients"
>
> Step 2: Know Where You Want To Go
> Where am I going?—"I want to be a small business owner with 50 clients who are all in my top platinum program and each are referring me 3 new clients a year."

In this example, it's possible that step two, because it's more detailed and specific, might cause you to feel nervous or anxious. If this is the case, then it's better to be less specific and have a "broader vision" in step two:

Step 1: Know Where You Are
Where am I?—"I'm a small business owner with 20 clients"

Step 2: Know Where You Want To Go
Where am I going?—"I want to be a small business owner with 50 clients."

So, in other words, be as specific as you can and *still feel good*.

STEP 3: TAKE ACTION

It's usually this third step that can become a bit of a stumbling block for some people. How do you know which action to take, right?

It's easy to look at others who are already successful and say something like, "Sure, it's easy for them. They know what to do."

Well, I have a big secret to share with you now.

Really, this is a HUGE secret and so make sure you're sitting down . . .

· ·

All self-made successful people—all of
them, each and every one—had NO IDEA
how they were going to get to the top of
their profession when they started out.

· ·

That's right. Countless successful people, from Bill Gates to Mary Kay Ash to Oprah Winfrey to Sam Walton and all those who have become successful in any sphere of life, did not know how they were going to achieve their success or what steps would get them there when they were at the beginning of their journey.

They did not know what to do anymore than you do. How could they have? When they were starting out, they didn't know what would work and what wouldn't work. They learned what worked and what didn't by trial and error and by taking action.

In reality, successful people end up knowing less about what to do and more about what not to do. Why? Successful people make more mistakes than unsuccessful people, and they're far more willing to fail than those who don't succeed, because they are more willing to take action.

In the end, you can't know which actions will lead to success, especially when you're in the early stages of running your own business.

So when I say, "take action," you might be asking yourself, "Well, what the heck am I supposed to do?"

The answer is . . . DO ANYTHING!

And of course, the caveat is "do" anything as long as you're feeling good. Take Intentional Action. After you have moved yourself to a more positive emotional place—by using any of the techniques you've learned from Train Your Brain—then DO ANYTHING!

And the fun thing about this exercise is you don't really have to concern yourself with WHAT you're going to do. Do you best to understand your industry and take action that makes sense, but then, as Nike would say . . . Just Do It! Seriously, take your best shot. Make your best guess!

TRY ANYTHING!

The reason I say, "do anything," is that when you feel good and take action, you're "creating energy" and this energy will produce an outcome that you'll be able to evaluate in the future.

And no matter how small this first step may seem to you, the action of doing anything will always reveal your next step.

But take that first small step. Do anything.

So that's the secret. Highly successful people were not certain how to get where they wanted to go when they started out, but they were willing to take action and try anything. And while you may not be certain how to get where you want to go, you can do exactly the same thing.

Feel good. Take action. Do anything.

Do you remember in an earlier section I said you do yourself a disservice by continually asking yourself questions such as, "What's wrong with me?" or "What's my problem?"

Well, if you want to better serve yourself then merely replace self-defeating questions with this simple one:

> *"What is the next small step I can*
> *take to move toward my vision?"*

STEP 4: EVALUATE THE RESULTS OF YOUR ACTION

Step four to getting where you want to go is to evaluate the *results* of your action. Bill Harris of Centerpointe Research Institute calls this the "Dr. Phil Step," where you ask yourself, "How's that workin' for you?"

After taking some action, no matter how small or insignificant it seems to you, examine or assess the outcome of your action.

Follow these three guidelines for evaluating the results of your particular action:

1. If you feel you've made progress, you might consider taking more of the same action.
2. If you didn't get the results you expected, consider alternative action.
3. If you've made progress but not enough, ask yourself how to improve the particular action to make it work better for you.

Whatever action you take, you are going to learn something, because learning is the natural result of taking action. You are going to learn what works and what doesn't work. Take enough action, and you'll quickly become an expert on the subject of action.

STEP 5: REFINE THE ACTION

Based on the evaluation in step four, you can now refine your action. Your refined action may or may not be any more effective for you, but this doesn't matter. If you continue to keep yourself in an emotionally positive place, and take action from there, you will most certainly get where you want to go.

This idea of taking action from a positive place is crucial.

Obviously, the more successful the action, the faster you'll get the results you want, but either way, don't just stand there. Do something, no matter what it is. This is the key.

Those people who wait and wait and wait to act never realize what works and what doesn't work. You never discover what works until you take action.

The point is, before any of us act, we're just guessing.

I'm not saying to go out and do a bunch of ridiculous things just for the sake of saying you took action—although even that is far better than standing still in almost every case. However, what I am saying is first put yourself in an emotionally positive place and then take your best action to move your business forward. It's that simple.

STEP 6: REPEAT STEPS 3, 4, AND 5 UNTIL YOU GET WHERE YOU WANT TO GO

That's right. This is the wash, rinse, and repeat step. You're always keeping yourself in an emotionally positive place before you take action and you're always evaluating the results of your actions and refining your actions until you get where you want to go. Enough said.

PUTTING ALL SIX STEPS TOGETHER

It's important to know that it's completely okay if your actions aren't exactly right all the time. In fact, they might be wrong, over and over again and maybe for quite some time. Eventually, you will refine your course and be successful because you've done the most important tasks—you've gotten yourself to feel good and you've taken action. That's Intentional Action.

It's the same as when a plane is traveling from Minneapolis to Mexico City. Technically, it's running off course most of the trip and the only reason it arrives at its targeted destination is because the pilot continually adjusts the course along the way.

And this is exactly what you'll be doing by putting all six steps together into a cohesive plan of action. You'll be making some mistakes, but you'll also be righting the course continually until the entire process becomes second nature. And eventually each action you take will pay huge dividends for your business. Isn't that exciting?

Remember, successful people succeed because of their mistakes.

Are successful people doing things the "right way"?

Not always.

Is there even a "right way" of doing things?

Probably not.

I'll be the first to admit, it's nice if you only make a mistake once. But if you're less worried about making mistakes and more willing to take action, you'll get where you want to go as a *direct result* of your mistakes and you'll get there quicker and easier.

If you adopt this type of attitude, from here on out, you won't be able to hold back from taking action! You'll be so motivated and fired up and you'll see anything and everything you do as a success!

"Good judgment comes from experience and
experience comes from bad judgment."

~ Chinese Proverb

You may continue reading or go to part two of this book and play with Mindware Experiment #19—Asking Better Questions: The Remix.

CHAPTER 38

WHERE YOU'VE BEEN

Whew! We've covered a lot of territory!

Before making a few final important points and wrapping up, I want to recap what has been covered in Train Your Brain.

First, we learned about the conscious mind, or "thinking mind," where every one of your thoughts originates—it's the part of the brain with which you are most familiar.

The conscious mind is what I playfully call the "mini sports caster" inside the brain, giving you a running commentary about every single thing occurring in your busy life. It's also the part of the brain you use when you focus and learn new information.

Then there's the unconscious mind, the part of the brain of which you are unaware. This part of the brain takes care of all of your bodily functions and you operate from your unconscious mind 95% of the time.

The unconscious mind takes the thoughts you've practiced in the conscious mind over and over again and stores these thoughts as beliefs—beliefs about yourself and the world around you.

Beliefs begin as conscious thoughts and are solidified into your unconscious mind by either agreeing or disagreeing with these particular thoughts. Emotions play the most vital role in forming your beliefs.

After your beliefs are stored in your unconscious mind, they form your "inside world picture." The way you behave in the world and the things you notice around you combine to form your "outside world picture." Your inside world picture and your outside world picture always match.

Then you looked at how most people are on the Cycle of Perpetual Sameness. You discovered how many people look at evidence or circumstances in their lives and react to those situations with an emotion. They then have a "self-talk" about those circumstances and cement those situations in the unconscious mind, which causes those situations to happen again and again.

You learned that less you rely on external events in your life to determine how you think and feel, the better chance you have for creating your own healthier, more productive inside and outside world pictures.

Then you delved into emotions and found that thoughts generate all your emotions. Your thoughts are "building blocks" necessary for forming beliefs in your unconscious mind. Emotion and feeling "attached" to your thoughts solidify or transform thoughts into beliefs in the brain.

In any given situation, your thoughts always precede your emotions—and never the other way around.

By using perfect language, you discovered how using simple words and phrases can help you change your inside and outside pictures of the world.

You made a decision to re-create your inside and outside world pictures by becoming aware of your thoughts and changing your self-talk using perfect language, Transitory Statements, better questions, and new stories.

You learned "negative" emotions are not only necessary but also, quite useful. Consistent recognition and acceptance of "negative" emotions makes you more aware of your good feelings and gives you the best chance for real movement and change.

I talked about emotional awareness as one of the most effective ways to manage your feelings. When you can bring all your emotions—both "good and bad"—into your conscious awareness, you learn that no emotion, no matter how self-defeating it may seem, can sabotage you in any way, shape, or form.

In the end, hopefully you learned that the most formidable "tool" to help you navigate your way through all your various feelings and emotions is your own thoughts.

You discovered emotion as the single most important clue for what you are thinking in any given moment and, hopefully, you began seeing your "feelings as signals" telling you to pay attention to your thoughts.

You uncovered a lot about the Emotional Scale . . .

You can only move one spot at a time along the scale because you can't go from anger to belief or from fear to joy all at once. Your brain is naturally wired to move only one step at a time along the Emotional Scale.

Many people rely on outside circumstances to determine their emotions and Ping-Pong back and forth along the Emotional Scale and, as a result, only experience small or minimal changes in their businesses.

Getting yourself to feel better, independent of external circumstances, helps create a more resourceful brain, help you to take better action, and helps move your business forward quicker and with greater impact.

Hope is "enough." Hope is the first purely positive place on the Emotional Scale, and "getting to hope" is when positive outcomes really start showing up. I also acknowledged that all of us become frustrated or less-than-hopeful from time-to-time running a business, but if you can just get yourself to hope and "maintain this feeling" consistently, success is guaranteed.

Another place on the Emotional Scale you understood more fully was "knowing." I addressed the concept of knowing from different angles because I wanted to show you that knowing—as opposed to clearcut emotions like fear or anger or frustration—is more difficult to define.

You learned that knowing is a feeling of certainty that "something great is on the way" even though you don't really have any evidence. You just . . . know.

And perhaps more than any other emotion, knowing doesn't just occupy your mind but might also be a sensation in your body—something stronger than any of your typical emotions, something "beyond belief."

Next you uncovered Intentional Action. You discovered that if you are feeling less than positive, you should do nothing. Do not take action in your business when you are in a less than positive emotional place. Instead, make an "intentional and conscious effort" to move to a more positive place on the Emotional Scale by using the Train Your Brain Mindware Experiments. Feel better first and then, and only then, perform any actions related to your business.

After you're feeling good, do anything! If you take action, you have results, and you know what works and what doesn't work. You're able to evaluate the action, refine the action, and continue to move toward your goal.

Of course, we all want to feel good all the time, but we know this is unrealistic, especially running a business. We know emotions are constantly fluctuating.

That's why simple and mindful ways of looking at your thoughts and emotions, "recognizing and accepting" each one of your feelings—the good and not-so-good—means you won't be spending so much time trying to "fix yourself" or, worse, getting into a destructive self-blame game.

And as a result of becoming being more emotionally aware, you'll have so much more positive energy to create your successful business and nourish your vibrant life!

You've discovered that Mindware Experiments help strengthen your mind muscles, keep your emotions positive and stable, and Train Your Brain for Success!

And because you're no longer letting all those circumstances beyond your control make you feel good or bad, you start managing all aspects of your life and business. And you feel good regardless of any circumstance in the world around you.

In the end, you're successfully navigating your way through the complex and unpredictable world of thought and emotion, using highly efficient tools to simplify this world and build the strongest case you can for your own success.

When people ask me the difference between hope, belief, and knowing, I like to explain it this way:

When we feel hope, it feels almost like a wish. We dream and want something good to happen, but we're not entirely sure it will happen.

When we feel belief, we feel pretty confident that it's going to happen. We're just not so sure *when* it will happen.

When we feel knowing, we're positive it's going to happen *so we don't care when*. We just . . . know.

After listening to or reading Train Your Brain, many entrepreneurs will tell me they're worried about beliefs stored in their brain, and feel these beliefs have a "mind of their own" and control how they think and act.

This is a natural concern, and I always tell people it's not really necessary to concern yourself with your beliefs. Instead, concern yourself with your "awareness." Because whatever you give your awareness to or anything you continually focus on, will always "show up" for you.

In the essence of Train Your Brain, when you consistently pay attention to your feelings, your emotional awareness will always tell you what you are thinking at a particular moment because your thoughts always precede your feelings.

Develop just a single flame in your mind, clearly defining your visions and desires by "listening" to your thoughts and thereby maintaining your emotional awareness . . . and I guarantee you, this one small flame will ignite and light up your entire life's path until nothing stands in your way!

CHAPTER 39

WHERE YOU'RE GOING

In closing, I'd like to leave you with one final story from Lou Tice, because I think it's a story that clearly demonstrates how our brains naturally work.

This story is about a little girl starting Kindergarten. When a child starts school for the very first time, most often the child's parents have been talking about and fussing over this milestone event for months and months before the child actually spends one second inside the school's walls. It's a truly exciting time!

Long before her first day at school, the little girl's proud parents will be saying things to her such as, "You're getting so big! Pretty soon you'll be going to go to school for the very first time! We're so excited for you! You're going to ride a big school bus! You're going to paint beautiful pictures at school and hear wonderful stories!" We're going to buy you a brand new backpack and fill it up with books!"

Even the girl's grandparents and aunts and uncles and big brothers and sisters will chime in, adding to all the excitement and anticipation surrounding this great event in her life.

The auntie will be driving the child to an event or an appointment and as they drive by the elementary school, the auntie will say, "That's your school! You'll be going there very soon!"

The grandfather will read a book and say, "Soon your teacher will be reading books to you at school!"

So naturally, when the first day of school arrives, we find our little girl sitting at the breakfast table. She's been sitting there since 5:00 AM, with her backpack on, eagerly waiting for her parents to wake up!

She's so excited! Wild horses couldn't keep this little girl from going to school!

Now let's imagine what would happen if the topic of going to kindergarten was never mentioned to the girl at all. What would happen if not one word was spoken to her about this milestone event? What if it was never discussed?

Imagine if the parents just woke the girl up one morning, dressed her, put on her backpack, and then sent her out to the bus stop, and simply said to her, "See you later. Have fun at school, Sweetie!"

The little girl would probably flip out!

Even if she did have a naturally adventurous spirit and manage to get on the bus without any waterworks, getting off the bus and entering the busy, chaotic atmosphere of the school, with so many unfamiliar faces and so many excited kids running around everywhere would likely send her on emotional overload. It's safe to say the little girl would become overwhelmed and either go into a shell, have a fit, or breakdown crying.

Even if the little girl makes it through this first day, it's a sure bet those same wild horses couldn't drag her back to that school tomorrow! She'd probably be too terrified to go back!

And why? The girl's inside world picture and outside world picture wouldn't match at all. Her inside world picture has her spending the days with her parents, driving with her auntie, and learning from books with her grandparents. Nowhere in her inside world picture is a school, teachers, unfamiliar faces, and hordes of kids.

But her parents did discuss going to Kindergarten for several months prior to her actual first day of school, and so she was able to imagine herself in a brand new situation, comfortably, safely, and prepared. She was able to imagine what it would be like and change her inside world picture.

All the anticipation swirling around in the little girl's head was not only preparing her for this big day. She was also feeling excited by the possibility. By the time the first day arrived, she was thrilled to be going to school! In fact, she couldn't imagine NOT going to school . . . it was now "normal."

The girl's inside picture of the world and outside picture of the world matched up perfectly!

And this is how your brain works. And it works the same way for all of us. When you use your own thoughts to imagine yourself in new or unfamiliar situations, safely and with positive anticipation, you will become, just like the little girl, thrilled by the possibilities. Do it often enough and your feelings will abound with excitement, anticipation and positive expectation! Continue to do it and the new situation begins to feel "normal."

Remember, what shows up in your life ALWAYS comes in response to what you're thinking and feeling.

If you feel good, with positive expectation, about a new life situation showing up for you . . . it will show up for you.

There is no other way.

This is your brain, trained.

This is the match you've been seeking all along!

This is your mind, aware.

When you exert consistent, conscious control over your own thoughts, the flow of energy created brings about a "momentum of emotion." The energy and excitement begins to feel natural to you, as though it's always been that way!

You will never go back to thinking and feeling as you did before!

Why would you?

This feels too good!

Carl Jung, when talking about creating change in our lives, once said,

> I am not what happened to me,
> I am what I choose to become.

So I ask you right now . . .

> What are you excited about?
> What are you anticipating?
> What are you expecting?
> Who are you choosing to become?

Remember to play with Mindware Experiment #20—Beyond Reason: Generating Your Own Positive Expectation in part two of this book and please visit http://www.trainyourbrainformore.com for free mantras, worksheets, and other useful material.

PART TWO

MINDWARE EXPERIMENTS

This section of the book contains all of the Mindware Experiments and so I wanted to say just a few things about them before you get started.

The Mindware Experiments are meant to get you stretching your mind muscles in many new, fun, and exciting ways!

This is . . . Train Your Brain . . . at work for you!

It's not a requirement to do all of The Mindware Experiments. Do the experiments that appeal to you and you can always revisit the others at a later time.

When you're playing with a Mindware Experiment, try to do it for at least 24 hours. You'll soon find that some of the experiments become part of your daily life and you will do them every day from here on out, but when you're first trying them out, whenever possible try to stay aware and conscious of them for at least 24 hours unless otherwise stated in the experiment itself.

Finally, in some of the experiments you're going to become much more aware of the thoughts you've been thinking and it will become very clear why you've been getting the results you've been getting in your business and other areas of your life.

Please try to go easy on yourself as you do these experiments. Try to be objective and open-minded with yourself. The experiments are not meant to be a reason for you to beat up on yourself with that rolling pin about your findings or your results. Try to look at your results objectively like a scientist would. This is why I named these exercises "experiments".

I think that name elicits a sense of adventure, curiosity, and playful attitude—all of which are beneficial and necessary to creating your own success. And, as with all experiments, just go ahead and try them. If you don't get the exact results you'd hoped for, go ahead and tweak it to your liking! Keep trying and playing and you will see your results change right along with your experiment.

Remember, all of your Mindware Experiments are works in progress . . . so is your life . . . and so are you!

One of the reasons The Mindware Experiments are so effective is because they provide the clear connection between our own thoughts and our results. They help open doors for you by training your brain to allow new information into your conscious awareness. This new information provides a shortcut for you by offering simpler and more effective ways to create success with less effort and less time.

Our first Mindware Experiment will illustrate the direct connection between thought and emotion and how you can use this close relationship to feel better in any moment.

With that, I'll close this section with a quote from Ralph Waldo Emerson. He said, "All life is an experiment. The more experiments you make the better."

Have fun with your first experiment!

MINDWARE EXPERIMENT #1

THOUGHTS CONTROL FEELINGS

Read through this exercise first, and then follow through on your own.

Let's begin . . .

Close your eyes.

Think about the biggest issue you face today, or something bothering you right now. Chances are you've already given this issue some thought, and so it's probably right there on the surface.

I want you to list, in your mind, all the reasons why you're upset about this particular issue. Don't hold back. Go on a little tirade if you like. Again, mentally list all the reasons why you might be feeling stress or anger about this particular issue.

With your eyes closed, start listing all your reasons. Do this for 30 seconds.

As you do, take a second to notice what type of emotion you are feeling now that you've made a conscious effort to focus on this issue.

Try to name the emotion or the feeling rising up inside you.

Are you feeling angry, frustrated, depressed, overwhelmed, stressed, upset? Or is it something else?

Next try to pinpoint where in your body you're feeling this emotion? Be as specific as you can. Is the feeling in your head? Neck? Shoulders? Chest, Stomach, or somewhere else?

Now open your eyes and "shake off" this feeling. If you need, take a deep breath and shake your body around a bit.

Now you're going to do a different exercise. Take another deep breath and close your eyes again.

This time think of one of your favorite places where you like to relax or even an imaginary place where you would like to relax in the future. This could be a beach or sitting in a hot bath or lying peacefully in a hammock under a beautiful tree or just relaxing in your favorite recliner. Take just a second and visualize yourself, "in your body" in this very relaxing place.

Take another deep breath. Take notice of your senses around this location in your mind. How does the air feel on your skin?

Take notice again . . . what smells are in the air? Pause for a minute. Can you describe the smells?

Take another deep breath. What textures or sensations are you feeling on your skin? Can you hear any sounds?

Take a deep breath and notice again the sounds and sensations. Describe these sounds and sensations.

Now breathe deeply and pay attention to the colors you see? Can you describe what you "see" in these surroundings?

Again, take note of the emotion you are experiencing. What are you feeling? Are you feeling relaxed or calm? Are you sleepy? Are you feeling peaceful? Happy?

And again, where in your body are you feeling this emotion? Can you pinpoint it to one area of your body?

Okay, you can open your eyes now. We call that going to your happy place.

Okay. I'm guessing you experienced two very different emotional states with these two visualizations.

The first exercise may have produced an emotion in your body such as stress, anger, worry, fear, or depression.

On the other hand, the second exercise most likely produced feelings such as relaxation, bliss, peace, calm, or joy for you.

No matter which specific emotions were generated in you, there is one important thing to note here . . . the whole time you did these two different exercises you were sitting in the same room, in the same chair, and in the same body.

The only thing that changed between the two different exercises was your thoughts.

Two distinctly different sets of thoughts "produced" two very different sets of emotions. Why?

....

Because <u>every</u> single emotion is
generated by a thought.

....

From now on, making a "simple conscious effort" to pay attention to this one fact will prove invaluable for facilitating positive change in your business.

MINDWARE EXPERIMENT #2

STAYING AWARE: WHAT THOUGHTS AM I THINKING RIGHT NOW?

Incorporating Train Your Brain into both your business and your life as a daily regimen will have you flexing new muscles in your brain; you'll focus more attention on your thoughts, emotions, and beliefs.

And these same thoughts, emotions, and beliefs—which may have confused you in the past—will now become "tools" to help you build a highly successful business quickly and effortlessly.

This is the real effect of Train Your Brain, the mind becoming a "powerful tool" for your success.

Thinking positively will become more "second nature" to you and, as a result, you'll find yourself working less while money and success flow into your business quicker and with much less work on your part.

Okay. Let's begin Mindware Experiment #2 . . .

For at least the next 24 hours, but you may choose to do it longer, as you go about your day, if you're feeling frustration or any other type of "counterproductive" emotion—and we all know what these sensations "feel" like—stop for a moment and ask yourself, "What thoughts am I thinking right now?"

When we're frustrated or angry it's easy to notice what thoughts are making us feel this way because these thoughts are typically right there on the surface.

Unfortunately, these thoughts often come spilling out of our mouths in the form of angry or irrational verbal outbursts. @$%^&★!

So when this happens, pause for a moment.

At that point, get your mind aware by paying close attention to your conscious mind. You will immediately notice a whole stream of thoughts inside your head making you feel this way. This "flow of thoughts" is the only evidence you need.

And this "evidence," is the next most important step in getting your mind more aware. By paying closer attention to what kinds of thoughts are in your head at a specific moment, you're finding the cause of a particular negative or counter-productive feeling inside you.

Keep paying attention to your thoughts. Remember, you will immediately hear a stream of sentences in your head that might sound like perfectly legitimate "reasons" why you are frustrated.

Good. You are now becoming more aware of your present way of thinking. Play around with these thoughts and try going to your happy place like you did in Mindware Experiment #1.

Visualize yourself in a relaxing place again and describe a special place in detail. When you do this, you will naturally "feel" your emotions shift toward the positive.

Now, just for the sake of experiment, see if you can think of something soothing to put in place of the angry thoughts. Try sentences like these . . .

"It will be okay."
"Things will turn around."
"I am already starting to feel better."
"I am already starting to relax."

Try it. Remember this is an experiment. Have fun and pay attention to your results.

Important note: This particular Mindware Experiment might not work the first time for you, but I guarantee if you continue doing this exercise, you will notice the feelings of frustration or anger going away or fading.

The most important thing is to take notice of your thoughts. This will increase your awareness, and it's another fun and exciting way to "train" your brain.

This exercise works anytime you have an uncomfortable emotion.

If you feel frustrated with traffic, or a computer issue has got you down, or a coworker has teed you off, or maybe one of your children can't seem to listen to you . . . pause for a moment first. Get a good handle on your feelings, and then pay attention to the thoughts inside your head at that very moment.

Getting yourself aware of which thoughts are causing you to feel angry or frustrated is the best way to begin thinking more in the "present moment." Maybe Carl Jung said it best,

....

Until you make the unconscious conscious,
it will direct your life and you will call it fate.

....

Remember . . . your conscious effort to become more aware of the direct link between thought and emotion is literally developing a newer way of thinking. Whether it's thinking more consciously, or more in the present moment—each of these choices keeps counter-productive thinking at bay; and it allows you more time to complete your constructive tasks. It also makes achieving your goal of building a highly-successful business much easier.

Okay . . . back to our experiment . . .

How might Mindware Experiment #2 play out in a real-life situation for you?

Well, let's say you have a computer problem. If you're running a business from home, this computer problems can really set back your day and sometimes multiple days.

NOTE: Insert your own particular experience regarding your business, friend, family, partner, or any life circumstance. Any negative experience works with this exercise.

So let's say the computer crashes or breaks down in some form or another. When you find yourself feeling frustrated, or angry, or any other negative or counter-productive emotions from a situation like this . . . apply Mindware Experiment #2 . . . and make a conscious effort to pay attention to what you're thinking.

Chances are you're probably thinking:

> "You have got to be kidding!"
> "I cannot afford to have this computer crash right now!"
> "This is making me crazy . . . what a hunk of junk!"
> "I've got better things to do than deal with computer issues today!"

So while you're completing Mindware Experiment #2, again, stop yourself for a moment, take a deep breathe, and ever so slightly, change your way of thinking so it sounds a little more like this:

> "Okay. I'm going to stop thinking these thoughts for just a minute."
> "I'm going to go to that relaxing place in my mind and I'm just going to try to think a different thought about this situation and see if I can generate a different emotion."
> "For starters, I could think that when this has happened in the past, I've always worked it out."
> "I know it may not be the best of situations, but if I breathe deeply, I'll get through it."
> "I'd even be willing to think that maybe something good will come out of it."
> "Maybe this is an opportunity for me to find a better system."
> "It will be okay."
> "Things will turn around."
> "I am already starting to feel better."
> "I am already starting to relax."

Simply changing the way you say things will generate different thoughts for you. This will naturally result in more productive emotions, and your previous negative feelings of frustration or anger will soften as you change the way you think about your situation. And even though you're changing your thoughts ever so slightly, I promise you will notice how you begin to feel better when you apply Mindware Experiment #2 to a frustrating situation.

And when you change the way you think about a situation, you now have a more resourceful mind, able to create more resourceful solutions.

Again, do this every time you catch yourself feeling a negative emotion.

Believe me, doing this one exercise alone will create an epiphany of sorts for you, because you will realize you don't have to feel like you're being held hostage by your emotions. This realization will catapult your business forward!

This will be an exciting time! You're beginning to make your own choices. You're gathering tools to keep you on track to build a financially-thriving business quicker than you ever imagined possible! And, ultimately, you'll find there is an "easier way" to build a successful business.

In the end, getting your mind more aware—by paying closer attention to your thoughts—means you can change your feelings any time you want or need.

Keep in mind, that in the same way you construct a house one brick at a time, the most effective way you build a successful business is by applying these smaller Mindware Experiments.

So applying these smaller techniques as opportunities arise in your day will give you a great head start. And you'll be able to respond more constructively to your day-to-day business.

These early experiments are the crucial first steps to training your brain. Some concentrated effort in the beginning lays the solid foundation for lasting success.

Have fun becoming more aware of how you think!

MINDWARE EXPERIMENT #3

OBSERVING THOUGHTS

You might remember in Mindware Experiment #2, you were focused on noticing when certain emotions arose and then you tried to identify the thoughts that caused those emotions.

Well, in this Mindware Experiment, you're going to continue in that same vein except this time you're going to do it in reverse. Rather than focusing on your feelings, I'd like to you to become more aware of your thoughts.

In this experiment, keep yourself in the **present moment** as much as you can. When a particular thought comes into your awareness, take notice of it right away. As you've learned, becoming more "mind aware" is the first step to making change.

Begin by concentrating on the thoughts you're hearing inside your head. Listen closely to the running commentary. What is that little newscaster is saying to you? Are you hearing any positive thoughts? Are you having any negative thoughts?

A lot of what you'll be hearing in your head is called "white noise," all those mundane, everyday conscious thoughts such as . . . "Don't forget to mow the lawn." . . . "Make sure I pack fruit with the kids' lunch." . . . "Turn the coffee pot off when I go to town." . . . "The dry cleaner closes at 4:30."

No need to pay too close of attention to these types of thoughts. Concentrate on thoughts with more emotional weight. They'll be easy for you to identify as they definitely differ from the white noise.

Do you notice any habits of thoughts in certain areas?

Is it time management or how busy you are?
Is it lack of money?
Is it personal relationships?
Is it confidence or self-worth?

Do you notice yourself chronically thinking about any area of your life in particular? Make note of these areas, especially if you are thinking worried, upset, depressed, or frustrated thoughts in any particular area.

When you do make a conscious and concentrated effort to listen to your thoughts, what you hear might not sound so good to you. So it's crucial, as you pay attention to your thoughts you never "judge" yourself. Just pay attention to your thoughts, and be objective with yourself.

As difficult as that sounds, please do try to remember, this is an experiment. Do your best to laugh at yourself and have some fun with it.

Now, phase two of Mindware Experiment #3 is the same as in the last experiment. Remember to see if the events and circumstances happening in the world around you (your outside picture of the world) match up with any of the phrases you hear "sounding off" inside your head (your inside picture of the world.)

This experiment will give you more practice at increasing your awareness . . . so as you're paying attention to the thoughts running through your head during this experiment, ask yourself this very important question . . .

Are my thoughts matching up with my outside picture of the world?

I'll bet you will find a match.

Remember, thoughts + emotion = beliefs and after a belief is formed, the unconscious mind is doing its diligent work as a tireless matchmaker for you—all without your asking—and you will find that these beliefs are driving the driving force behind what is appearing in your life.

Simply put, the only real way for you to gauge whether your inside and outside pictures of the world are directly linked together is becoming aware of the "evidence" in your life. In other words, is what you're saying to yourself coming true or showing up in your life?

I know you will find plenty of evidence that reveals a direct correlation between what you are thinking and what is "happening" in your life.

What I hope to accomplish with this book is to help you see the direct link between the thoughts inside and the events in your outside world.

And when you discover this unmistakable connection, you'll experience a huge "AHA!" moment!

You'll experience this incredible rush of feeling like something clicking. And you will immediately begin to see positive shifts in your business and your life.

This is making change and interrupting the cycle.

Looking inside yourself and finding out what makes you tick helps you make change at the conscious level. This is important because all your thoughts, emotions, and beliefs get their start in the conscious mind. It's only when these are left unchecked in the unconscious mind that they begin to affect your life automatically and, seemingly, without your knowledge.

So pay attention to your thoughts. Thinking more consciously, more actively, and being more aware gets you in the present moment as much as possible, which ultimately paves the way for making change.

Increasing your conscious awareness by looking inside, and making good, solid decisions based on new information about yourself, will positively transform your business and your life!

So have fun with this experiment and have fun paying attention to your thoughts!!

MINDWARE EXPERIMENT #4

TURN IT AROUND

You may remember me mentioning in a previous chapter that we use mantras in two ways.

1. Interrupting the Cycle. In the heat of a moment when you catch yourself using negative language or engaging in a negative self-talk, you can change your self-talk immediately and implement a perfect language mantra that is positive and better reflects the outcome you'd like to achieve.
2. Ongoing. You can create one powerful, personal, perfect language mantra to say repeatedly during your day on an ongoing basis, whenever you think of it.

In Mindware Experiment #4 called Turn It Around, you're going to really play with the first area . . . interrupting the cycle.

To do this experiment, pay attention to your thoughts. If you catch yourself having self-defeating or negative thoughts about your business or any area of your life, stop, pause for a minute, and then turn it around . . . meaning, turn those thoughts around to the positive.

Pay close attention to any recurring themes. Do you notice any particularly chronic negative or counter-productive thoughts?

When you become aware of repetitive negative thoughts, apply the four guidelines for perfect language to the new positive statement:

1) Make your statement in the positive.
2) Make your statement as though it has already happened or already been resolved.
3) Make your statement believable.
4) Go for the positive emotional impact. Avoid wishy-washy language.

Noticing your negative or self-defeating thoughts or statements and turning them around to the positive immediately will have a lasting effect.

Here is an example of how to implement this Mindware Experiment.

Let's say you are in your office and you look at the clock and think, "I can't believe how many hours I've been at this. I'm killing myself with this business." You want to catch yourself right there. Is this the image you really want your unconscious mind to find a match with? Definitely not, right?!

So now you can play around with some of your new statements until you get closer to using the perfect language. Here's how that might sound and feel:

> "I wish I wasn't working so much." (No, that doesn't feel right.)
> "I wish I didn't have to work at all." (No, not that either.)
> "I wish I was independently wealthy." (Still grasping)
> "I am independently wealthy." (Hmm . . . don't really believe that one.)
> "I am happy that I love what I do." (Hey, much better, and it feels better, too!)

Saying "I am happy that I love what I do," feels better and is a much better picture to match than "I'm killing myself with this business", right?

Does saying this last phrase make you work reasonable hours immediately?

Not quite, but your ability to turn it around—making a clear, concise, positive statement to counteract the negative thoughts—will help you feel better, and the more often you feel better, the more often you will make better choices. This consistent reprogramming of your unconscious mind changes your beliefs (your inside picture of the world) which ultimately changes your outside picture of the world.

So now that you've found your new, more productive way of thinking, say these words or phrases a few times—silently or out loud, it doesn't matter. You really want to let the emotion generated by your words put a smile on your face! Feel good about what you are saying.

Turning it around is another simple mind tool to effectively help you be more aware that what you "say" can literally transform how you feel and what you believe.

Keep playing with this Mindware Experiment. Catch yourself throughout your day when you're having less than productive thoughts and always take a few moments to turn it around.

Have fun turning around your thoughts . . . and your business!!

MINDWARE EXPERIMENT #5

CREATE YOUR OWN MANTRA

In the last Mindware Experiment we used mantras to "interrupt the cycle" and turn it around. Now it's time to tackle the second method for using mantras. In Mindware Experiment #5, you will create your own mantra.

In working with entrepreneurs all over the world, I've learned that sometimes it's easier for people to discover what they want, if they first reveal what they don't want.

So, in learning what you want for your business, phase one is to complete these sentences.

> If I could change one thing about my business, I would change . . .
>
> The biggest frustration I have with my business right now is . . .
>
> The skill I most want to learn for my business is . . .
>
> If I could have a magic pill to fix one thing about my business right now, it would be a pill to . . .
>
> I know I could be successful at this business if only I . . .

Answer them quickly with the first answer that pops into your head. To make this Mindware Experiment easier for you, there is a "discover your mantra" worksheet available for download at http://www.trainyourbrainformore.com.

After you've answered those questions, it should be obvious to you what you'd like to fix in your business, so now go on phase two of this process and answer these questions.

> What would it look like if the problem was gone?
> What would I be, do, or have if the problem was fixed?

The answers to these two questions will give you the basis for your first mantra.

As you're creating your first mantra, remember what you've learned about perfect language.

1) Make your statement in the positive.
2) Make your statement as though it has already happened or already been resolved.
3) Make your statement believable.
4) Go for the positive emotional impact. Avoid wishy-washy language.

Pay close attention to the fourth guideline . . . go for the positive emotional impact. This is the most important guideline of all. You will know if you have a good mantra, if it makes you feel good.

Often the most successful mantras for people who practice Train Your Brain are very short, powerful, general statements. Examples of these types of mantras would be:

> "Business is booming!"
> "I'm a money magnet!"

"Money is flowing to me!"

Or even better . . . "Money is flowing to me in great quantities!"

If you can get more specific and still feel good, that's great, but always remember that the most important aspect of your mantra is that it must make you feel good.

Sometimes creating a rhyming mantra can be fun. An example of this would be . . . "Business is booming. My life is improving."

A really simple method for creating a mantra is to add the words ". . . is so easy" to the end of any skill you'd like to develop. Here are some examples of this type of mantra:

"Picking up the phone is so easy!"
"Growing my business is so easy!"
"Making money is so easy!"
"Managing my time is so easy!"

If you'd like to some ideas to get you started, go to http://www.trainyourbrainformore.com and enter your email address. We'll send you 200 ready made mantras, as well as a workbook for helping you with these Mindware Experiments . . . including this one.

Create one mantra to begin and after you've decided on a mantra that you like, start repeating it over and over, either out loud or silently to yourself. Simply repeat the mantra whenever you think of it throughout your day.

Some people will set an hourly alarm on their phone as a reminder to say their mantra periodically throughout the day. Repetition of your mantras will create amazing outcomes.

Believe me, when you say your new mantra dozens or hundreds of times a day in the same way followers of Train Your Brain do, you will see evidence that your mantra is working so quickly it will make your head spin! I promise.

If for any reason you don't get some quick evidence with your mantra, simply review your wording and see if you can make it tighter and more effective. Creating your mantra is a process and you will tweak and change it as you go along. Striving for "perfect" language is very important, but always be aware of your emotions as you create your ideal mantra.

Mantras that evoke positive emotions improve your chances for success. So if your mantra isn't making you feel much emotion, dump it. There are millions of little phrases and sayings you will come up with, easily.

You will always know if a mantra is working by evaluating how you feel. Emotions are your barometer. If you feel good when you say your mantra, then it's working!

Have fun, and experiment! I know you'll find a mantra that works!

When you find your mantra that works, this might feel like magic to you, but it's not.

You are simply making a conscious effort to think in new ways that loosen up the filter in your brain. This allows new information into your conscious awareness and brings fresh and exciting opportunities into your business!

Have fun creating your own mantra!

MINDWARE EXPERIMENT #6

BOMBARD YOURSELF WITH POST IT NOTES

Perhaps you've noticed by now that your Mindware Experiments don't require any tools in the literal sense. Your biggest and best tool for building your business is your mind. Know this and you will build a financially thriving business quickly and with much less effort than you originally thought possible.

In working with clients at The Mind Aware, I've found that the easy to implement techniques actually get implemented and therefore they actually get results. This is why our Mindware Experiments are so easy to implement.

Truthfully, other than increasing your conscious awareness, a little added focus, and a willingness to try some new ideas, getting the positive results you'd like for your business is far simpler than you might have previously thought.

The only "tool" you really need is your mind. It's the strongest tool you possess if you want to build your own financially viable business quickly.

That said, Mindware Experiment #6 actually does require a pen and a stack of post it notes. Here is how it works:

On your post-it note, write one simple mantra, which reflects what you want for your business in the near future.

Remember what you've learned about perfect language and creating effective mantras:

1) Make your statement in the positive.
2) Make your statement as though it has already happened or already been resolved.
3) Make your statement believable.
4) Go for the positive emotional impact. Avoid wishy-washy language.

Also, keep in mind shorter phrases, and more direct statements work better. Remember this is something you expect for your future. Be believable, but bold and clear.

Even though you are imagining or visualizing and writing a mantra for something you expect to happen in your future, you are still writing your statement as though this has already happened.

Here are some examples from a variety of industries:

> "My calendar is full with appointments!"
> "I sold $2,000 in product this month!"
> "I had my best month ever!"
> "I sold my first house!"
> "It's so easy to pick up the phone!"

Okay. Now write the statement you chose on at least a dozen post-it notes. Place the post-it notes all over your house, in your car, and anywhere you will see them often. You can't post too many, so go ahead and place as many post-it notes as you can.

There will be a temptation to write down two or three different statements, but it's important for the purpose of this Mindware Experiment, to stick with one phrase.

You certainly can make minor adjustments to the statement so they remain fresh and interesting for you, but stay within the same topic and outcome for each post-it note statement.

MindAlert: You might feel silly posting these notes all over your house where everyone can see them and you'll likely take some ribbing, but the results will be worth it if you stick this one out.

Go ahead and leave your notes up for several weeks to a month—or as long as you like.

Soon after the post-it notes are up, your statements will become "familiar" to you and you may no longer "see" them, but your brain will continue planting these messages into your unconscious mind.

One member of my team was an expert at booking parties. She always had a full calendar. But no matter how hard she tried; she just could not sponsor people into her business on a regular basis. After a year and a half with the company, she had only two people on her team . . . so she decided to give the post-it note experiment a try.

She started placing post-it notes all over her house. Her statement said . . .

> "It's so easy to recruit!"

Every so often she would add a, "woo hoo," at the end of her statement on the post it note. It would read . . .

"It's so easy to recruit . . . woo hoo!!

She laughed at herself as she put up the notes, thinking the exercise was a bit silly, and as the weeks passed, she no longer even noticed the notes on the walls.

But, lo and behold, after she posted her notes on the walls, over the next six weeks, she sponsored 11 new people into her business!

Think about that! After sponsoring only two people on her team in a year and a half, she had more than quadrupled her sponsoring numbers in only six weeks! Amazing! All from "silly" post-it notes!

This is just another incredible story reinforcing the idea that your brain will literally transform your business for you. And sometimes all it takes is putting up a few post it notes!

Have fun posting positive notes everywhere!

CREATE YOUR OWN
TRANSITORY STATEMENT

For this Mindware Experiment, you will implement your own personal Transitory Statement. As with any of our Mindware Experiments, if you decide to try this one, make sure to implement it for at least 24 hours, but feel free to continue for as long as you like.

The first step in Mindware Experiment #7 is to ask yourself these three questions . . .

1. Are there mantras I've tried which "sound like a lie" and might work better as a Transitory Statement?
2. Are there any deep-seated beliefs I have about myself I'd be willing to soften a bit with a Transitory Statement?
3. Are there any recurring negative thoughts I have about myself that might be turned around with a Transitory Statement?

If you answered yes to any of these questions, you may want to try this Mindware Experiment. Remember there are three types of Transitory Statements for you to try:

1) Keep the image, but change the message.

2) Link the change to an event.

3) State the change as though it is in progress.

There are worksheets to help you with the process of creating your own Transitory Statement at http://www.trainyourbrainformore.com.

When creating your Transitory Statement, play with each of the three methods and see which one feels best. Whichever one feels best, will work best.

After you have crafted your new Transitory Statements, just use it like you would a mantra. Say it many times a day, whenever you think about it.

In addition, whenever you catch yourself having negative thoughts, you can use Transitory Statement principles to turn those thoughts around.

As I mentioned earlier, whether you're talking with others or having certain thoughts in your head, you will quickly realize the words you "choose to use" in your day-to-day life are crucial to changing old beliefs held in your unconscious mind.

And creating a new, healthier belief—will ultimately depend on the choices you make regarding what "new language" you can bring into your conscious awareness.

It's really amazing how just a few words can get you feeling a whole lot better about your business; speeding up the process positive change in your business!

Creating Transitory Statements and implementing them on a regular basis will really help to drive home the importance of positive emotion in creating change in your life.

You'll see how even imperfect language can be effective when it generates positive emotion inside of you. As always, the words you use are only as beneficial as the good feelings they generate.

I cannot say it enough . . . positive emotion is everything!

I personally use a lot of "imperfect language," but it still works to create positive change in my life because it generates strong, positive feelings in me.

For example, one of my all-time favorite mantras is "I'm unstoppable!"

This mantra certainly doesn't adhere to the guidelines I mentioned earlier about creating effective mantras using perfect language. This statement not only has the prefix "un" in it—which is a no-no—it even has the word "stop" as part of the statement!

In the context of perfect language, this statement is far from ideal. However, the phrase makes me feel good! I always feel like a racing freight train when I say it. I feel like nothing stands in my way when I say, "I'm unstoppable!"

The point is, you can create a perfect language mantra, but if you don't feel good when you say the words, it won't work to reprogram your unconscious mind. So, until you can implement a perfect language mantra and feel good, a Transitory Statement will do the trick.

Always trust your feelings, because good, productive feelings show that you're on the right track!

Have fun creating and implementing your Transitory Statements!

MINDWARE EXPERIMENT #8

ASK A BETTER QUESTION

For Mindware Experiment #8, you're going to use your brain's natural tendencies to answer your questions to your advantage. You're going to craft a question for your unconscious to answer.

Here is how it works . . . first, you think of something you'd like to have in your life. For this experiment, it needs to be specific and tangible. Here are some examples of things you may want to have or do:

- Increase your business by 20%
- A new car
- Lose twenty pounds
- Add ten people to your team
- A prize or attain a level of achievement
- $100,000 net income
- Be a bestselling author
- A million dollar business

After you know what you want, you then craft a "how" question using this introductory phrase:

How could I _____?

The word "how" puts your unconscious mind into problem-solving mode for you. Using this formula, our topics listed above would be crafted into questions like these:

- How could I increase my business by 20%?
- How could I get a new car?
- How could I lose twenty pounds?
- How could I add ten people to my team?
- How could I earn (prize of level of achievement)?
- How could I make $100,000 net income?
- How could I be a bestselling author?
- How could I create a million dollar business?

For a worksheet to help make crafting your powerful question easier, please go to http://www.trainyourbrainformore.com.

Next, after you have crafted your powerful question, you will plant it into your unconscious mind and so I want to give you a few guidelines for this process.

1) Craft only one question.
2) Unlike a mantra, you will not repeat the question over and over. Instead, you will try to think of it multiple times throughout the day, but only once or for a brief second. Do you remember earlier how I mentioned that sometimes no matter how hard you try, you can't remember a name, place, or where you put an item, but then you always recall it after someone says, "forget about it and it will come to you?" This is how this Mindware Experiment works too. You are NOT trying to answer the question. You are thinking the question once, implanting it, and then "forgetting" about it.
3) Set a phone notification to remind you to implant the question throughout the day.

One more very important point about this particular Mindware Experiment . . . "how" questions don't always feel good and as you know, at The Mind Aware we really want you to feel good. Success comes from feeling good and so this is why you may want to take some time when you craft your question to arouse some good feelings inside of you regarding the object of your desire. You can actually do that with another "how" introductory phrase:

How would my life look if I _____?

Put together with our topics from earlier, those powerful questions would look like this:

- How would my life look if I increased my business by 20%?
- How would my life look if I got a new car?
- How would my life look if I lost twenty pounds?
- How would my life look if I added ten people to my team?
- How would my life look if I earned (prize of level of achievement)?
- How would my life look if I made $100,000 net income?
- How would my life look if I became a bestselling author?
- How would my life look if I created a million dollar business?

Get the juices flowing on the object of your desire because then when it comes time to implant the question in your unconscious mind you will already have some positive emotions around the subject.

As you start to practice this Mindware Experiment, you're going to notice your brain kicking in and wanting to answer the question immediately. It will take a little conscious awareness on your part to control your conscious mind from wanting to give you a whole list of answers. Just remember, this experiment works when you "set it" and "forget it."

And I'll tell you why . . . let's say you crafted the powerful question, "How could I create a million dollar business?" Immediately when you think that question, you may get a jolt of good feelings. You may remember that your mind pictures the subject of the sentence immediately and as your mind "hears" the powerful question, the image of a million dollar business will arise just as quickly as a pink elephant. The image of the million dollar business will give you a rush of good feelings.

However, if you ponder the question for too long, what quickly happens is your conscious mind will start chiming in about all the reasons why your idea is stupid or impossible. Why it will never work and so on. You don't want to allow that to happen and so remember . . . you are not trying to answer your powerful question. You are thinking about it, implanting it, and then forgetting it. You are allowing your unconscious mind to reveal the answer to you.

Keeping your mind off of your question effectively opens the door for your unconscious mind to get into problem-solving mode and work on answers for you.

And that's exactly what will happen.

What happens when you put your unconscious mind into problem solving mode is that all those opportunities you have missed or overlooked in the past will pop up for you seemingly out of the blue. You will feel inspired about a new marketing idea, which has been there all along, but you never noticed it. Or you find yourself in a conversation with an old friend you haven't seen in years who gets excited about your business and partners with you in some way.

Seem farfetched? It's not. This is a direct result of training your brain. And it's tempting to underestimate the power of your mind, but when

219

you get amazing results, and you will, you will never undervalue how easy it is to transform your life simply by the way you think!

Asking a self-defeating question benefits no one. On the other hand, asking a better question is one of the best ways to use your brain's natural tendencies to answer questions to your advantage.

Your new line of questioning and its limitless prospect of success will soon have you realizing all things possible can become real.

Have fun asking better questions!

MINDWARE EXPERIMENT #9

ELIMINATING AUTOMATIC NEGATIVE MESSAGES

Have you ever had a friend or colleague who seemed to shoot down new ideas automatically? This could even be a well-meaning friend, but he or she just had a habit of saying, "you can't do that", along with a long list of reasons why a particular idea won't work.

Well, sometimes, even your own automatic negative response seems to pop up in your conscious mind just when you feel like you're heading toward more positive thinking. This automatic negative message is a common knee-jerk reaction, a kind of counterweight to feeling good.

You've probably seen this in countless movies. Faced with a dilemma, the character has a "little angel" perched on one shoulder, and a "little devil" on the other, both giving their advice.

Similarly, as an entrepreneur or small business owner, you may have an automatic negative message that makes it sound like an argument in your head. It might sound something like this:

Your Positive Message	Automatic Negative Message or "Knee-Jerk Reaction"
"I'm financially abundant."	"No, you're not."
"Money flows easily to me."	"Yeah, right."
"My business is growing quickly."	"This is so stupid."
"I easily attract customers."	"Except they have no money."

Is this familiar to you? Have you ever heard that second negative voice speak up after you've said something positive to yourself?

Well, if so, don't worry. These types of exchanges are common. Automatic negative messages are easy to identify and quite predictable, but you'll be happy to know that they are also easy to remedy.

Before we get started with Mindware Experiment #9, I'd like to remind you of our previous Mindware Experiment explaining Transitory Statements. You may remember that Transitory Statements are worded in such a way they don't wake up the little devil on your shoulder.

However having said that, Mindware Experiment #9 will give you a few additional tools for eliminating automatic negative messages. When you identify a particularly stubborn negative message, which keeps popping up in your mind, try some of these techniques:

- Neuro-Linguistic Programming or **NLP:** First, "listen" to the automatic negative message in your head. What is the negative phrase you are hearing? Repeat this phrase over and over, silently or out loud, making sure the automatic negative message gets softer and softer in volume each time until the automatic negative message "disappears." Next, "turn it around" and think of a positive phrase to replace it. Use the same process for your positive message. Repeat it over and over, this time making sure the positive phrase becomes louder and louder each time. Repeat this process several times.

- Visualization: When the automatic negative message creates a negative image in your mind, use visualization so this negative image "spins away" from you out into space and disappears. Then, again, turn it around with a corresponding positive image in your mind and visualize it spinning toward you, growing in size, vividness, and clarity.

- Silly Voice: This one is fun! Repeat the automatic negative message in a silly voice, like the voice of Goofy from Walt Disney, or Elmer Fudd. You may want to say this one in your head in case someone's listening. The "silly voice" should make you smile and chuckle. End this technique by saying a corresponding positive phrase with your normal voice, confidently and happily or if you are having fun with this, you can even make it the voice of your favorite cartoon hero.

- Set to Music: Go back to the first technique, and when the sound of the automatic negative message has completely diminished in volume and you've replaced it with a more positive-sounding message, set your new positive message to music. This creates an "earworm" or jingle effect inside your head. If you're going to have a song stuck in your mind, it might as well be one with a positive message.

As you apply these techniques you'll diffuse or minimize the power of the automatic negative messages. In turn, the second half of each exercise allows you to increase the power of your new, positive message.

Automatic negative messages are only problematic if you allow them to persist, which you will see happening less and less as you continue this path of positive self-talk. Try to keep in mind you are more aware of your negative thoughts now and that's a good thing. The better you

Dana Wilde

feel, the less likely you are to tolerate any negative thoughts. Knowing this makes eliminating automatic negative messages a breeze!

Play with this Mindware Experiment. Anytime you have a knee-jerk response or an automatic negative message, try these suggestions for eliminating those thoughts. Play around with your new positive message too and I know you'll find a favorite method from those listed here.

Have fun eliminating those automatic negative messages!

MINDWARE EXPERIMENT #10

CREATE YOUR OWN BECAUSE STATEMENT

In Mindware Experiment #10, you craft your own Because Statement to add to the end of your mantra.

Remember, when you add a because statement after your initial positive message, the unconscious mind automatically starts justifying why your initial positive message is "true" and accepts its validity without question.

For a worksheet to help you craft your Because Statement, please go to http://www.trainyourbrainformore.com, but here are a few guidelines to remember:

1) Make sure your Because Statement is also a productive, positive outcome—something you either hope to achieve or have already achieved.
2) Be mindful of your wording. It will appear in your outside world picture.
3) Your mantra and your Because Statement can be completely unrelated topics.

4) Follow the same guidelines in crafting your Because Statement as you would a good mantra:

    a. Make your statement in the positive.
    b. Make your statement as though it has already happened or already been resolved.
    c. Make your statement believable.
    d. Go for the positive emotional impact.

Again, when you add a Because Statement after your mantra, the unconscious mind automatically starts justifying WHY your initial positive message is "true" and accepts its validity without question.

So, just like people in the Xerox line in our previous story, you can take advantage of the power of the word "because" very simply. If you even add the words, ". . . because I'm saying this mantra" to the end of your mantra, your unconscious mind will immediately accept the validity of your mantra. Just like in the story, your mind does not care which reason you pick for change. It will accept any reason wholeheartedly.

Jump in and have fun creating your Because Statements!

ASKING A BETTER QUESTION: THE SEQUEL

You now have a good handle on the power of the unconscious mind to solve problems for you, and you're keenly aware that Because Statements make your mantras much more effective. Next, in Mindware Experiment #11, you'll learn to combine better questions with Because Statements to create a powerful tool for you.

As you learned previously, questions instantly put both the conscious and unconscious mind into problem-solving mode.

In addition, you might recall from Mindware Experiment #8 that "how" questions should be left to the unconscious mind to answer. When you think about a "how" question with your conscious mind, it doesn't always feel good, and so this is why it's better to let your unconscious mind reveal the answers to your "how" questions.

However, there is a type of question which is perfectly suited for your conscious mind to answer and that is "why" questions.

Whereas answering "how" questions can hamper your business by adding unnecessary stress to your life, "why" questions often elicit a more positive emotional response.

You can gauge this for yourself with a quick comparison. Let's say you want to earn $100,000 a year from your business. If you let your conscious mind ponder this goal for too long, you might come up with a series of of "how" questions that sound like this:

> How am I going to do that?
> How can I talk to that many people?
> How will I learn everything I need to know to do that?
> How will I handle the workflow?
> How will I get that much product shipped?

You no doubt can feel the stress these questions induce. This is why how questions are better left to the unconscious mind to answer.

On the other hand, try taking the same desire or the same goal, to earn $100,000 a year from your business, and instead of asking, "How?" ask "Why?" What happens when you ask "Why?"

Asking "Why?" naturally elicits a "because" answer from you.

A because answer is your mind's way of giving good reason and validation for a particular positive outcome to show up for you . . . and you may have also noticed that it feels good. You bypass all of the stressful feelings produced by "how" questions.

After you ask "Why?" your "because" answers might sound like this:

"I want to earn $100,00 a year from my business . . . Why? . . .

". . . BECAUSE it will make me feel good."

". . . BECAUSE I like the idea of more money coming in."

". . . BECAUSE I will feel like I'm making progress in my business."

". . . BECAUSE it will be fun to have more money to spend."

". . . BECAUSE I want to use the extra income to buy a car."

". . . BECAUSE it will be cool to attain a goal I've set for myself."

. . . and so on and so on.

Notice when you ask the question, "Why?" you are able to combine better questions with Because Statements you are able to use words to your advantage to create a powerful tool for change!

And good feelings—even when they come from a simple word such as "why"—always produce amazing results for your business!

So for Mindware Experiment #11 write down your own desire or goal. Write down what you want and then ask yourself "Why?" Use the guidelines you've learned for perfect language and create a long list of answers to that question, which will immediately generate a ton of good feelings for you.

You can even do this Mindware Experiment without the pen and paper. The next time you are waiting at a stoplight, just declare out loud what you want and then ask yourself "Why?" and then answer that question with a whole list of Because Statements.

Play around with this experiment. Go ahead and figure out what you want and have fun answering "Why?"

MINDWARE EXPERIMENT #12

TELL A NEW STORY

Mindware Experiment #12 unfolds in three steps.

Step one, start paying attention to all the stories you're telling others around you. What stories do you tell your family, your friends, your co-workers, and others around you?

You'll quickly find out the "stories" you're telling others are often the same stories you're telling yourself. Pay close attention to the stories themselves as well as the feelings they generate.

Step two, if you find yourself telling stories that don't make you feel so good and you don't want these negative feelings to persist, simply ask yourself,

"Is this the story I want to be telling?"

Asking this question is another great opportunity for you to "turn it around," and tell a new story. It's also a great opportunity for you to turn off the "automatic pilot" type of thinking.

And whether you choose to tell a new story or decide to keep on telling the same story by staying on automatic pilot, keep this in mind . . .

whatever story you are telling right now will come into your life again and again.

Step three, if you so choose, craft a new "story" which better represents what you'd like to see in your outside world picture. When crafting the story remember the rules of perfect language as well as the rules for crafting Transitory Statements and Because Statements. Craft a new, powerful story and repeat it to yourself often!

Let the curious scientist inside you go to work and have fun with this experiment and always remember whatever makes you feel good will work. Keep playing with the story and changing it as you like until you achieve the outcome you desire.

Have fun telling a new story!

TRAVELLING THE EMOTIONAL SCALE

In Mindware Experiment #13, you are going to change your line of thinking so you can move away from negative or counter-productive feelings—whether it's hopelessness, frustration, or doubt—toward more productive places such as hope, belief, or knowing.

You are going practice "moving" yourself along the Emotional Scale. And again I'd like to acknowledge my appreciation for Abraham-Hicks for my own personal education on this technique. Here are the steps for executing this Mindware Experiment:

1. Identify your emotion. Where are you on the Emotional Scale? Remember, this feeling is your "signal" and it will always indicate to you what you are thinking.
2. Be aware of your thoughts. Pay close attention to the corresponding thoughts that created this particular feeling. Remember, your thoughts always create your emotion. Don't beat yourself up for having this feeling, regardless of how bad or negative it feels. You just want to see the direct connection between your emotions and thoughts, and how they work hand-in-hand.

3. Make a decision to "move yourself" along the Emotional Scale. For example, if you're feeling fear or worry, you know one step over is anger. In order to move yourself emotionally in that direction, you must first make a decision that you want to stop feeling fear and that you would like to generate feelings of anger.

4. Start intentionally thinking thoughts that correspond to the next emotion on the Emotional Scale. To expound on the example, you would want to intentionally "choose" thoughts that sound and feel angry. You would literally choose to get mad about some aspect of the situation (currently making you experience fear.) Keep generating angry thoughts in your mind until you actually start to "feel" angry.

5. Experience the "better" feeling. Experience the "relief" that comes with making the shift to the new emotion. In the example, the feeling of anger is more active than the feeling of fear or worry. You will feel a sense of relief by feeling anger and you will have intentionally moved yourself emotionally to this place of anger. You will want to stay with this feeling for a short while—a few minutes—but soon you will be ready to make the next move on the Emotional Scale.

NOTE: When you experience a new feeling, it will only feel good or give you that sense of "relief" for a short period of time. In our example, when you get that first rush of anger, it will feel great . . . like you're taking your power back, but if you stay angry, soon it will feel terrible. This is why in this experiment, you want to stay with the emotion for a few minutes, but then move on to better feeling emotions.

6. Make the next move on the scale using steps one through five, if you so wish.

You can apply this strategy to any feeling on the Emotional Scale. You can just start where you are and move to the next spot on the scale.

THE EMOTIONAL SCALE

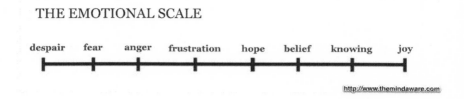

By implementing this Mindware Experiment, you will learn how to become completely emotionally independent of any external circumstance in the world around you.

When you do this, you'll realize there's no good reason to hold onto those nagging, counter-productive feelings for days. You'll also see that you can change your feelings instantly, by changing your thinking, if you so choose. And the best part is, you'll see all of this can be done without much time or effort, which means you'll never have to Ping-Pong back and forth on the scale ever again!

Have fun intentionally creating your emotions!

MINDWARE EXPERIMENT #14

WHAT IS KNOWING?

For Mindware Experiment #14, each and every time you're faced with an important task, which needs to be accomplished or carried out as it relates to running your business, simply ask yourself these two questions:

1. Can I trust in the process or systems?
2. Have others done it successfully?

The first question, "Can I trust in the process or systems?" could also be asked in these ways:

> Do I have examples that the system I'm wanting to use works?
>
> Do I know of a method that works for others?
>
> Is there a technique that I trust to work?

The next question, "Have others done it successfully?" could also be asked in these ways:

> Have others accomplished what I want to accomplish?
>
> Do others possess some special talent or magical power, or
>> did they just learn certain skills, which helped them,
>> accomplish certain tasks at hand?

If another person "learned" how to accomplish something,
do I think I can learn how to accomplish this, as well?

Asking these two simple questions will help ease any fear, frustration, or doubt about whether you can accomplish all the things necessary to produce positive outcomes for your business. In addition, it will give you the sense of relief that things will work out. Use Mindware Experiment #14 to help you to develop your own sense of "knowing" and take your business all the way to the top!

Have fun moving yourself to the emotion of "knowing."

MINDWARE EXPERIMENT #15

BEYOND BELIEF

Most of us don't give ourselves enough credit for all we understand about the world, or about our own lives. We don't give ourselves enough credit for all of the things we know.

We've come to depend on evidence beyond our control and simply wait for all the "good signs" to appear. So when we run our own business, or any new endeavor, we go into it with anxiety and apprehension.

So remember, as you Train Your Brain to manage worry and fear and doubt, you're building your own case for success. You're deciding to examine all the good evidence in your life. You're creating a feeling that nothing will stop you from learning what you need to learn to build a financially thriving business. You're building a case that you know you will succeed.

As I said earlier, you already have plenty of good, positive evidence.

The more you think about "what you already know," the more easily you can go beyond feelings of hope and belief to confidence, certainty, and knowing. And when you get yourself into this "state of knowing" more consistently, your business will sky rocket!

You accomplish this by continually asking yourself,

> What do I know already?
> What are my past successes?
> What am I particularly good at?

Think about it. There was a time when you couldn't send an email, or tie your shoes, or wash laundry or prepare a meal for yourself. There are thousands of tasks you've already learned. Maybe you can play a musical instrument. Or you have a hobby you are proficient at doing. Maybe you make a darn good batch of chili. Maybe you can drive a car or ride a bicycle or dye your own hair or change your oil or speak another language or are terrific at crossword puzzles.

So why, then, should learning the skills to run a successful business be any different for you, right?

For Mindware Experiment #15, a pen and paper is all you'll need. I want you to make a list of some of the things you know—things that at one time you couldn't carry out, get done, or complete and are now able to do without much effort.

You might want to think of accomplishments in your adult life. If you went back to the time of your infancy, obviously this would be a funny—and extensive—list. So just think in broad strokes for this experiment. In other words, what does past experience show that you've "learned"?

Think about aspects of your life that have become "ordinary" for you. Maybe it's cooking certain foods, riding a bike, sending emails, or driving a car. Though these kinds of tasks may seem mundane to you now, you still had to learn how to do them at first.

Think about any job you've had and how quickly you became proficient at it. Think about hobbies and skills you've mastered. Are you proficient at music, language, computers, writing, sewing, woodwork, sports or yoga?

List anything you had to learn and can now say with great confidence, "I know how!"

Examining your past accomplishments and all the things you already know makes running a successful business just another learned set of skills.

So for this next Mindware Experiment, that's exactly what you'll be doing. You'll be moving yourselves into a feeling of knowing.

Have fun making your list of the things you KNOW!

MINDWARE EXPERIMENT #16

THE HOPE EXERCISE

Seeing the title of this Mindware Experiment, you might be thinking I've spent all this time talking about knowing so why am I going back to talking about hope? Isn't this a step back on the Emotional Scale?

This is a step back, but for good reason.

Let's face it, who doesn't want to have a sense of confidence and knowing about their business twenty-four hours a day, seven days a week? We all do, right?

However, the reality is that you will experience peaks and valleys with your emotions. This is natural. Knowing there will be good days and not-so-good days is a big part of successfully navigating your way through the Emotional Scale. Being human means experiencing the full spectrum of our emotions.

Although being in a place of knowing is great, I certainly don't want you to think that the only way for you to be successful in your business is to sustain this feeling of knowing. In fact, that's not true at all. It's not realistic and it's not necessary.

You may remember me mentioning earlier that feeling hopeful is "enough" to gain traction and success in your business. Many people are surprised and relieved to learn this.

When you get to hope on the Emotional Scale—and remain there as consistently as possible—you can accomplish great things quickly and easily, even if you never make it to feelings of knowing or joy.

So why is hope . . . enough?

Hope is the first "positive" feeling on the scale, and it's the first place from which you'll begin to see good, solid results in your business.

I've said throughout this book that by doing your Mindware Experiments and applying what you learn to your business, you will create noticeable shifts and positive outcomes for your business. This will happen easier and with less effort than you ever imagined!

I know from training thousands and thousands of entrepreneurs, the ability to create noticeable shifts in business and produce those amazing financial results is never more evident than with this Mindware Experiment.

Most small business owners don't struggle with feelings of despair, fear, or anger about their businesses for extended periods of time. They may briefly visit negative or counter-productive emotions but, usually, those who stay stuck in fear or worry usually give up on their businesses.

On the other hand, many entrepreneurs dip in and out of frustration and hope quite a bit, Ping-Ponging between the two emotions. Typically, they have small successes quickly followed by small setbacks; which is why many businesses grow incrementally instead of by leaps and bounds.

So this is why getting to hope is so important, and why it's enough. In my experience, when people stay in a feeling of hope for longer periods of time, they begin seeing a strong pattern emerge. It emerges as positive change and substantial business growth.

You really want to avoid or eliminate the emotional Ping-Ponging between frustration and hope.

You really want to get into a "place" of hope on the Emotional Scale, and sustain this feeling as much as possible.

The Hope Exercise is really simple. It's similar to the exercise when you traveled the Emotional Scale, except this time you're focusing only on the movement between feelings of frustration and hope.

To execute this experiment, whenever you feel frustrated or overwhelmed, just pause, take a deep breath and start coming up with phrases or statements beginning with the the words . . .

"I hope."

Your statements might sound something like this:

"I hope I start to feel better."
"I hope I find a way to get my business moving."
"I hope I find a method that makes my business easier."
"I hope I get some people to buy my product."
"I hope someone walks up to me out of the blue and buys something."
"I hope I make a lot of money in this business."
"I hope I attain my goals."
"I hope I start to feel more positive."
"I hope I my business grows this year."

"I hope things improve."

"I hope I can think of another hope sentence."

When you've said your hope statements a few times, pay close attention to how you "feel." If you find your emotions dipping back into frustration again—consistently applying your hope statement wards off counter-productive thinking right away. It will get you quickly back into that hopeful feeling again!

Keep saying your new "hope phrases" until you experience emotional movement towards genuine feelings of hope.

Another important note: When you first start using hope statements you'll find, though you're making hopeful or optimistic statements, they might sound and feel more like frustration than hope to you. However, if you say your statements for several minutes, you'll begin to feel your emotions soften, your mood lighten, and you'll immediately start feeling better.

This is a natural process because, again, thoughts equal emotion, and these "better thoughts" translate into "better feelings." This is more good evidence that this is working successfully for you! What evidence, you ask?

The evidence is . . . you feel good!

Have fun playing with your hope statements!

243

MINDWARE EXPERIMENT #17

CHANGE YOUR BREATHING

By now, I hope it's becoming clear how important emotions are for creating change in your business and your life. And you already know that when you feel overwhelmed or stressed you tend to make more mistakes and create more work for yourself.

Emotions are crucial ingredients for generating good, positive change. And because feelings of stress and aggravation are common emotions for anyone running a business, most of our Mindware Experiments focus on helping you shift your emotions. However, because entrepreneurs are often some of the busiest people around, we wanted most of those experiments to help you feel better with very little effort.

You've probably heard the advice: "If you're feeling angry, take a few deep breaths and calm down."

Well, that's EXACTLY what you're going to do for Mindware Experiment #17!

You're going to take a few deep breaths, calm down, and "change your breathing."

Have you ever thought, really thought, how important breathing is to you?

No? Well, listen to this.

Without food, you can last for weeks.

Without water, you can last for days.

Without breathing oxygen, you'll die within a few minutes.

Breathing is truly vital for your survival. It's your only means of getting oxygen to your body. If the supply of oxygen is compromised in any way, this has adverse effects on your entire body.

And because of increasing demands on our already-complicated lives, stress dramatically affects the way we breathe. So we're pouring all our energy into combatting these feelings, and stress can cause us to breathe shallow or in quick, short bursts. We might also end up forgetting to breathe altogether for short periods of time. Stress can literally starve the brain of oxygen!

As a result of this added stress, fatigue affects us more than it did before. And we're quicker to act out of frustration and anger, so irritability and moodiness occur more often.

So if stress strongly affects our emotions, and breathing is necessary for our survival, then why do we take breathing for granted?

The body's breathing is done unconsciously. We don't need to "remember to breathe" because our unconscious mind executes this crucial task for us.

Bringing the act of breathing to the conscious level grounds you in the present moment, relaxes you, and adds more oxygen to your brain. I'd like you to make a conscious effort to "attend to your breathing." Get your mind aware of the importance of breathing by incorporating breathing techniques into your daily life.

Scientific studies have proven that breathing techniques help with many facets of our lives, especially with stress-related problems.

Experts in spiritual yoga, meditation, and martial arts have known for thousands of years that simply changing how we breathe greatly affects how we feel. Breathing techniques elevate our emotions, which energizes our body mentally and physically, and facilitates general well being.

Breathing deeply and slowly may not make your emotions "jump into bliss" on the Emotional Scale. But as you concentrate on getting more oxygen into your body through breathing techniques, like the one found here in Mindware Experiment #17, this will relieve a whole lot of stress for you.

You want to use your conscious mind and focus to get yourself breathing more slowly, more deeply, and more effectively.

Breathing techniques keep stressful feelings at bay as you try to keep up with the demands of your business, while also trying to navigate your feelings and continue making positive movement along the Emotional Scale.

For Mindware Experiment #17, when you find your focus wandering, or you feel rushed, angry, frustrated, overwhelmed, worried, busy, annoyed, or any other stressful or negative feeling, take a few moments to relax, breathe deeply, breathe slowly, and center your being.

Count five seconds as you inhale and five more seconds as you exhale, for a total of ten seconds per breath. If you repeat this exercise six times, it will only take you one minute. You will feel better and literally change your outlook on the world. Repeat this exercise as necessary throughout the day.

For extra benefit, set an alarm on your phone several times throughout the day to remind yourself to do this exercise and watch the impact it has on your mood, your results, and your outside picture of the world.

When you're taking part in this breathing exercise . . .

You're in total control.

You're doing it because it's simple.

You're doing it because it takes so little time and feels so good.

It focuses you in the present moment.

And . . . all this extra oxygen . . . boosts your energy!

Increases your alertness!

Reduces your stress!

Makes you feel great!

And the best part is, you can start right now with Mindware Experiment #17. Take a deep breath in for five counts and then exhale for five counts.

Have fun breathing deeply!

MINDWARE EXPERIMENT #18

CHANGE YOUR BODY LANGUAGE

You've probably heard a thing or two about body language. If you see someone standing up straight with shoulders back and head lifted high, you sense they feel confident in what they are saying and how they feel about themselves.

Conversely, if they are slouching and holding their head down, you wonder if they are feeling a little blue or out of sorts because their "body language" is a giveaway.

Most of you can look at a friend or family member and immediately gauge their mood without much effort. You can literally tell by their body language how they are feeling.

Here's something less discussed: the concept of body language in reverse. In other words, can you change your mood by changing your body language?

Well, let's find out.

You can try this fun Mindware Experiment right now.

Whatever you're doing, stop for a minute, and look upward. While you have your eyes focused upward, smile!

Now try to think of a negative thought.

Bet you can't do it. Go ahead. I'll wait.

Isn't it nearly impossible to feel bad when you do this?

Simply the act of lifting your eyes upward and smiling immediately puts you in a better frame of mind!

So, again, here's a fun experiment you can play with anytime.

Anytime you feel low energy or you're feeling a little down, start by standing tall and throwing your shoulders back!

Next, lift your eyes upward and put the biggest, goofiest grin on your face that you can manage!

Next, you can start bouncing back and forth from one foot to the other, almost like a dance.

MindAlert: You might feel funny doing this, but the sillier and goofier you can make the face and the funkier the dance, the faster this technique works!

Go ahead. I dare you to do this for thirty seconds without cracking up! It's an instant mood lifter! And you'll also notice that you have more energy when you're done!

There are countless things you can do to make yourself feel better in any given moment. And many of these fun techniques demand very little effort.

Tried-and-true methods—listening to upbeat music, reading inspiring quotes or motivational material, writing a list of things you appreciate— are always handy standbys. The important thing is that you're taking steps toward feeling better.

And now that you understand the importance of feeling good, and how this produces tremendous positive results for your business, feeling good will become a priority in your life!

Whether you're changing your breathing, traveling the Emotional Scale, smiling, making a goofy face, dancing a jig, listening to upbeat music, or just playing with the cat or dog, you'll start to find that more and more of your time is spent on feeling good!

Have fun changing your body language, smiling, and being silly!

MINDWARE EXPERIMENT #19

ASKING BETTER QUESTIONS: THE REMIX

Now that you understand Intentional Action, it's the perfect time to start combining asking questions with taking action. Applying Mindware Experiment #19 will help you focus your action on more productive ways to run your day-to-day business.

Remember the question from earlier, "What's the next small step I can take to move toward my vision?"

Think about this question for a moment. Doesn't saying this question make you feel good? And doesn't the anticipation of endless possibilities excite you to take action?

Beyond feeling good, simply asking this question naturally makes it easier to decide which action step you should take next.

This Mindware Experiment helps reinforce how powerful questions can be in moving yourself emotionally and creating positive outcomes for you and your business. In Mindware Experiment #19, you are going to take the idea of asking better questions to another level.

You will move your business forward by combining better questions with action. Here's how it works . . .

Start with a goal you have in mind. Let's say you want to build a business where you have a 1,000 customers, or any other similar goal.

Think about how the actions you take on a day-to-day basis would improve if you'd consistently asked yourself "better" questions such as these:

- What would someone with 1,000 customers do to handle this situation?
- What books or literature would someone with 1,000 customers read?
- What would someone with 1,000 customers want to learn?
- What would someone with 1,000 customers do to schedule time more wisely?
- What would someone with 1,000 customers do to follow up with customers?"
- What would someone with 1,000 customers do to connect with other business professionals?"
- What would someone with 1,000 customers be thinking about?"
- What would someone with 1,000 customers be doing right now?"

Can you see how your actions might change if you were "thinking" like the type of person who had already attained your goal? Can you see where it might cause you to take different actions as well? You can insert your own goal into the following "better question" framework:

- What would someone with _____ do to handle this situation?
- What books or literature would someone with _____ read?
- What would someone with _____ want to learn?

- What would someone with _____ do to schedule time more wisely?
- What would someone with _____ do to follow up with customers?
- What would someone with _____ do to connect with other business professionals?"
- What would someone with _____ be thinking about?
- What would someone with _____ be doing right now?

To make this exercise easier, you can download a worksheet at http://www.trainyourbrainformore.com.

I recently heard from a woman who implemented this experiment and focused on these types of questions as a technique to move her business to a higher level of success.

She'd been in business for many years and was making reasonably good money. And she wanted to take her business to the million dollar level. In order to make this happen, she knew she had to "shift" her mindset, or way of thinking.

So she decided to try asking herself better questions.

She started thinking of herself as the owner of a million dollar business (even though she wasn't there yet). Then, she started asking, "What would the owner of a million dollar business do in this situation?"

When she found herself surfing the web just to pass the time, she began hearing a voice in the back of her mind asking, "Would a million dollar business owner be doing this right now?"

And the same question kept coming up when she'd spend time watching silly TV shows or, frankly, any meaningless activity—both in her business, and in her life: "C'mon, seriously, would a million dollar business owner be doing this?"

Soon she started noticing time and energy she normally spent on meaningless activities was now being channeled into her business. She now saw activities with her kids, husband, and friends as quality time.

Simply by asking herself "better questions" over and over, this already successful woman saw every area of her life continually improving. She felt confident and had more time for people and, even though she wasn't literally at the million dollar level yet, she began seeing herself as a successful million dollar business owner.

Every aspect of her business was affected by asking better questions. She became proficient at focusing on the MOST productive tasks each day. Procrastination became a thing of the past. She easily did what needed to be done each day, and almost every action paid huge dividends for her business.

And, as you might guess, just two years after starting to ask herself these better questions, her business went over the million dollar mark.

Isn't that a great story? It showcases the real power behind asking better questions and, more importantly, it reveals how "combining questions with action" can catapult a business to another level!

Give this Mindware Experiment at try and watch the results for yourself. Think about your goal and start asking how a person who's attained that goal might think and act. By focusing on actions that successful people might or might not take to move their business towards greater success, you are framing all your subsequent actions from that person's perspective.

Have fun asking better questions AND taking better action!

MINDWARE EXPERIMENT #20

BEYOND REASON: GENERATING YOUR OWN POSITIVE EXPECTATION

Before you conduct your final Mindware Experiment, I want to stress the importance of staying relaxed about your business and, more importantly, have fun doing these experiments.

All of the tools and methods in this book are designed to get you feeling good, which sometimes will even mean putting down this book, cranking up the music, and dancing or participating in some other activity that brings you joy!

Your final Mindware Experiment ties in nicely with our closing story in that it is going to help you to generate positive expectation in your life.

This Mindware Experiment requires a pen, a piece of paper or notebook and roughly ten minute of your time. You can do this Mindware Experiment one time or every day for an extended period of time or as you need it.

To do this experiment, write a sentence that represents what you "want" at the top of a clean sheet of paper. This is not a mantra and so it's not necessary for it to be in perfect language. It's simply a desire or declaration of something you'd like to see come to pass in your life. You want to write this desire in one sentence. This particular sentence or phrase might sound something like this:

"I want $10,000 in the bank."

or

"I want more time with my family."

or

"I want to be a Senior Director in my company."

or

"I want a new car."

or

"I want to be happier."

or

"I want to weigh 150 lbs."

or

"I want 50 clients in my business."

The possibilities are endless and again, just write a simple sentence stating what you want.

Next, underneath that sentence on that same page (and on the entire back page if you choose to keep going), write down all the reasons why you EXPECT this situation to come to pass. Why do you expect it to happen?

Notice I said . . . expect . . . WHY do you EXPECT to it to happen for you?

Not the reasons you *want* it to happen.

Or the reasons you *hope* it to happen.

Not even the reasons you *believe* it to happen.

You are writing down the reasons you EXPECT it to happen.

It's so important to write down all of the reasons why you expect it to happen because as you are writing down all the reasons, you'll naturally begin feeling an acute sense of expectation and excitement welling up inside of you!

And you may have already figured out you will be putting our friend, the word "because" to work in this exercise as well. You may remember that that word "because" automatically helps your brain "justify" why something is going to happen and then helps you to make it so.

Remember as you do this Mindware Experiment that you may have reasons that relate to "action" steps you take in your life, as well as "emotional" reason. For example, your page may look like this . . .

I want to make $10,000 a month in retail sales.

I expect this to happen . . .

. . . because I am approaching at least one new prospect a day.

. . . because I am getting better at picking up the phone.

. . . because I am doing more trade shows.

. . . because I have a new product I'm excited about.

. . . because I'm learning how to think more positive thoughts.

. . . because I'm doing this exercise every day.

. . . because I'm getting better at maintaining positive energy.

. . . because I'm spending more time with positive people.

. . . because I feel better about my business every day.

. . . because I know it's on the way.

I'm sure in reading the description of this exercise you can already feel the power behind it. Do this exercise anytime you need a boost in your business. Conduct this experiment every day for 30 days on the same general goal and, I promise, the results you will see will blow your mind!

Enjoy this final Mindware Experiment and have fun creating your own positive expectations!

ACKNOWLEDGMENTS

I am thankful to so many people who have helped to make this book a reality, starting with my family, who've empowered me from the very beginning. Katherine Fritz, Wade Kirby, and Erin Wallace, I appreciate that you have believed in me throughout my life and supported my decisions, no matter how ridiculous the idea or path may have seemed to the average person.

I also thank you for bringing Bernie Fritz, Martha Kirby, Clay Wallace, and Samantha Sack into my life. It's difficult to imagine my life without them or their encouragement. They are all true blessings in my life.

This book has evolved from decades of study of some of the greatest thought leaders of our century. The ideas and concepts in this book have been greatly influenced by, and not limited to, Carl Jung, Napoleon Hill, Wayne Dyer, Jerry and Esther Hicks, T. Harv Eker, Louise Hay, Lou Tice, Richard Bandler, Deepak Chopra, and Bill Harris.

As this book has taken shape, so many people have been a part of assisting me in honing my message. I am grateful for John Capecci who was the first to help me take my ramblings and put them into some type of structured order. His input directly impacted the clarity of the final audio version which carried over into this book.

I'm also thankful for Susan Iida Pederson who gave the entire project a facelift by helping me to cut out the fluff and restructure it into the two-part book you see today. She has been a gift in my life.

And Antoinette Caswell who went over the entire project with a fine tooth comb ... three times ... to make sure that every typo, grammatical error, and punctuation mishap was caught.

And I can't possibly fully express my appreciation for Richard Sauerer. First, he brought his gift of writing to this project by taking my seedling concepts and grounding them, so they are now more accessible. This process took the better part of a year. In addition, throughout this entire endeavor, he has supported me and our furry babies so that our household has truly become a place to create and grow. It's because of his nurturing spirit that we continue to flourish and words truly do not suffice in expressing my gratitude for all he has done.

I also wanted to give a shout out to all of the fantastic people at Balboa Press. It's hard to imagine I've been working with their team for almost two years now. Literally dozens of dedicated Balboa Press professionals have had a hand in this project in some way or another and many more to follow as we continue to spread the message of Train Your Brain. I'm so grateful for the day I chose them for this project.

In addition, I want to thank all of the dedicated, talented people I work with at The Mind Aware, with a special thank you to Desiree Wolfe. Every movement is only one crazy person with an idea until the second person gets on board. You helped make Train Your Brain and The Mind Aware a movement and I truly appreciate all you do.

Last, but not least, I want to thank all of the followers of Train Your Brain and The Mind Aware. It's been your willingness to implement The Mindware Experiments and watch your own brains create amazing outcomes that has allowed this project to exist at all. Your courage, desire, curiosity, ambition, and sense of adventure have made it all possible and I couldn't be more pleased to be on this journey with you all.

I want to express deepest thanks to everyone who has had a hand in this project. I am truly blessed.

Made in the USA
Middletown, DE
30 December 2020

30478897R00163